Critical Guides to German Texts

2 Frisch: Andorra

Critical Guides to German Texts

EDITED BY MARTIN SWALES

FRISCH

Andorra

Michael Butler

Professor of Modern German Literature
University of Birmingham

Grant & Cutler Ltd
1994

© Grant & Cutler Ltd 1994

ISBN 0 7293 0371 3

First edition 1985
Revised edition 1994

Der andorranische Jude is reprinted from
Max Frisch's *Tagebuch 1946-1949*. Copyright
© 1950 by Suhrkamp Verlag, Frankfurt am Main

I.S.B.N. 84-401-2135-0

DEPÓSITO LEGAL: V. 528 - 1995

Printed in Spain by
Artes Gráficas Soler, S.A., Valencia
for
GRANT & CUTLER LTD
55-57 GREAT MARLBOROUGH STREET, LONDON, W1V 2AY

Contents

For Maureen

Preface

Max Frisch's work, and *Andorra* in particular, has attracted a very large number of commentators over the last quarter of a century. In the face of such sustained critical attention, a further study of *Andorra* can hardly hope to break substantial new ground. Instead, I have tried to see the play as clearly as I could and, wherever possible, set fresh emphases. My indebtedness to other scholars is expressed in the Select Bibliography, but I would like to mention especially Wolfgang Frühwald, Peter Pütz, Walter Schmitz and Erich Wendt whose work on *Andorra* has decisively influenced mine.

I would like to thank the Suhrkamp Verlag, Frankfurt am Main, for permission to quote from Frisch's published work. I owe a special debt of gratitude to the British Academy for a research grant which enabled me to visit Switzerland, to Walter Obschlager of the Max Frisch Archive, Zurich, for his courtesy and helpfulness, and to Mary Davies for typing a less than ideal manuscript with great speed and accuracy.

Michael Butler
Birmingham, Autumn 1984

Preface to Second Edition

Max Frisch's death, on 4 April 1991, deprived European culture of a distinctively humane voice. Paradoxically, the recent collapse of totalitarianism in eastern Europe and the Balkans has brought in its wake a dangerous instability and the tragedy of civil war. Once again the veneer of civilisation has been shown to be depressingly thin. I am pleased that the need for a second edition of this book indicates that Frisch's exemplary study of fear and prejudice is still being widely read in schools and universities, for the message of *Andorra* has lost none of its urgency.

Michael Butler
Birmingham, Summer 1994

Note on References

References to Frisch's work are taken from the standard Suhrkamp edition, *Gesammelte Werke in zeitlicher Folge* (1976), 6 volumes. (This edition is textually identical with the simultaneously published *Werkausgabe Edition Suhrkamp,* 12 volumes.) Roman numerals refer to volume, Arabic to page. *Andorra* is printed in IV, 461-560. References to secondary literature take the form of an italicised number relating to the corresponding item listed in the Bibliography, with page references added where appropriate. The reference *MFA* signifies that the item is lodged in the Max Frisch Archive of the Eidgenössische Technische Hochschule, Zurich.

1. Context and Theme

Although Max Frisch's writing career stretches back to the early 1930s — his first published work, a short essay on the problems of acting entitled 'Mimische Partitur' appeared in the *Neue Zürcher Zeitung* on 27 May 1931 — it was not until 1945, when he was already thirty-four years old, that his name began to be noticed. This was only in part due to the fact that Switzerland was an isolated island of democracy during the Second World War, surrounded by the fascist Axis powers and their fellow travellers. For Frisch's work itself was surprisingly empty of political resonance during these critical years for Europe and moreover offered little evidence of the quality to come. This is not to say that Max Frisch was by temperament apolitical or kept his head wilfully in the sand; rather does it seem that the chaotic horror of the war seemed too problematical, too vast to be either opposed or encapsulated in the written word. Instead he saw his early writing as an attempt to articulate alternatives, not in the spirit of escapism, but in the awareness that this was at least one valid way of asserting human freedom in the face of tyranny. However, in an essay published in 1945, *Über Zeitereignis und Dichtung*, Frisch showed himself perfectly aware of the dangers he was exposed to, the sense of impotence to which his country's historic principle of neutrality inevitably led:

Der Krieg geht uns im höchsten Grade an, auch wenn er uns verschont. Unser Glück ist ein scheinbares; wir sind nicht imstande, es wirklich zu genießen inmitten eines Leichenfeldes, am Rande einer Folterkammer, wir hören die Schreie, aber wir sind es nicht selber, die schreien, wir selber bleiben ohne die Tiefe des erlittenen Leides, aber dem Leiden zu nahe, um lachen zu können; unser Schicksal scheint die Leere zwischen Krieg und Frieden, ein

Nichtganzvorhandensein, ein Warten, eine Ohnmacht im
scheinbaren Glück, unser Ausweg ist bestenfalls das
Helfen. (II, 285f)

Indeed, with the benefit of hindsight Frisch himself later
classified his creative work of the period up to 1945 — the
novels, *Jürg Reinhart* (1934) and *J'adore ce qui me brûle oder
Die Schwierigen* (1943, revised and reissued in 1957 with title
and subtitle reversed), the delightful, if slightly sentimental,
'Träumerei in Prosa', *Bin oder Die Reise nach Peking* (1945),
and the first stage play, *Santa Cruz* (1944, premièred 1946) — as
'Fluchtliteratur' (*1*, p.24). All these works centre on intensely
private issues: the problems of human relationships, the crisis of
personal identity, the creative individual in conflict with
bourgeois society. They seem in retrospect a deliberate attempt
to cling to traditional themes and traditional forms of expression
as an antidote to the momentous pressures building up on
Switzerland's frontiers, pressures of which Frisch had first-hand
experience in his periods of duty as a military conscript in the
Swiss army, and which he recorded in his first diary, *Blätter aus
dem Brotsack* (1940).

The year 1945 brought an inevitable turning point. With the
collapse of Hitler's Germany and the dreadful revelations of the
concentration camps, Frisch saw himself as a writer confronted
with a challenge of immense proportions. His profession of
architect (the practical study of which had been forced upon him
by his father's death in 1932) must have seemed a peculiarly
symbolic activity for any intellectual facing the problems of that
time: Europe lay in ruins, tensions between the Allies were
already clear and the task of reconstruction appeared an almost
overwhelming one despite the great burst of energy released by
the restoration of freedom to so many millions, not least in
Germany itself. For not only the major cities, particularly of the
Third Reich, had been destroyed; European culture itself, which
had after all spawned the nightmare of fascism, seemed severely
if not permanently compromised. No one felt this crisis more
keenly nor expressed it more clearly than the Swiss neutral
Frisch whose own cultural identity was so intimately bound up

with German and the German language. In a major essay of 1949, *Kultur als Alibi*, Frisch described his personal predicament in memorably succinct terms:

> Wenn Menschen, die gleiche Worte sprechen wie ich und eine gleiche Musik lieben wie ich, keineswegs gesichert sind, Unmenschen zu werden, woher beziehe ich fortan meine Zuversicht, daß ich davor gesichert sei? (II, 340)

The appalling results of National Socialist ideology had in effect profoundly shaken his faith in his own humanity. And yet paradoxically Frisch's initial response to the end of hostilities had been a play (his second, although the first to be produced), *Nun singen sie wieder* (1945), which was essentially a plea for tolerance between victors and vanquished. Written, it should be noted, some months before the Nazis unconditionally surrendered, *Nun singen sie wieder* is directly derived from the spirit of the eighteenth-century Enlightenment as exemplified in one of Germany's greatest writers, Gotthold Ephraim Lessing. Indeed, it is a curious but telling fact that Frisch's play and the finest dramatic poem of the Enlightenment, Lessing's *Nathan der Weise* (1779), were among the first dramas to be produced in Germany when the theatres re-opened in 1946. Yet despite the fact that Frisch's play is apparently rooted in such naive humanism, characteristic of much of the initial response to the prospect of peace and before the Cold War had developed its depressing contours,[1] *Nun singen sie wieder* does not evince a facile optimism — quite the reverse. Frisch's message is, in fact, couched in terms of a sombre warning that men and women will be tempted to reject their experience, that they will blindly strive to restore the old, dangerously defective structures. This attitude is captured in the words of the widow Jenny: 'Mein einziger Trost: daß wir alles wieder erbauen, so wie es war...' (II, 135) — a response to the past which will reappear in a bitterly ironic form in *Andorra*.

[1] As an example of the change of mood a mere four years later, see Klaus Mann's article, 'Europe's Search for a New Credo', *Tomorrow*, 8, no. 10 (June 1949), 5-11.

Nevertheless, despite his fears and acute insight into the depths of the contemporary malaise, Frisch did reaffirm the need to recapture the principles of classical humanism, the belief that the human individual is the measure of all things and that he can determine his own future creatively if his unique worth is only recognised and protected. The expression of such a philosophy remains not surprisingly a sceptical one, and indeed Frisch's idiosyncratic brand of 'sceptical humanism' becomes the hallmark of all his mature work and the source of its inherent tensions and characteristic irony. In the immediate context of the post-war period, however, Frisch's emphasis on individual human dignity as rooted in the ability to *choose* (see the *Tagebuch 1946-1949*, II, 488) brings him close to the existential philosophy of Jean-Paul Sartre. And indeed the prestige of French thought in its foremost representatives, Sartre and Albert Camus, reached its apogee in the 1940s and 1950s. Partly due to their inexorable insistence on individual responsibility in a world which had just witnessed its abdication in favour of collective madness, and partly due to the active role both French thinkers had played in the Resistance (the proof, it seemed, that philosophy and commitment were not after all irreconcilable opposites), existentialism dominated post-war intellectual debate and clearly influenced Frisch as it did — with rather different results — his fellow countryman Friedrich Dürrenmatt (who at the time was planning to write a doctoral thesis on the father of all existential philosophies, Søren Kierkegaard).

With their promise of a radically new start, Sartre's confident assertions in *L'Existentialisme est un humanisme* (1946)[2] were bound to strike a common chord. Arguing for the supremacy of existence over essence, for example, Sartre declared boldly:

> Il n'y a pas de nature humaine, puisqu'il n'y a pas de Dieu pour le concevoir. L'homme est seulement, non seulement tel qu'il se conçoit, mais tel qu'il se veut ... l'homme n'est rien d'autre que ce qu'il se fait ... L'homme est

responsable de ce qu'il est. Ainsi, la première démarche de
l'existentialisme est de mettre tout homme en possession de
ce qu'il est et de faire reposer sur lui la responsabilité totale
de son existence. (p.22ff.)

It is perhaps hard to recapture the dramatic impact of such
words or the thrill of Oreste's ringing cry at the end of *Les
Mouches* (1943): 'Tout est neuf ici, tout est à commencer', in the
immediate conditions of post-war Europe. But clearly what
attracted Frisch and so many of his contemporaries to this brand
of existentialism (see, for example, Alfred Andersch's autobio-
graphical story *Kirschen der Freiheit* (1951)) was the uncompromising assertion of individual liberty and dynamism, the
refusal to accept the concept of fatality, whether demonic or
historical, in human affairs. Above all, the fascinating rejection
of the fixed contours of human personality seemed to offer the
chance of a radical break with the past. Although it would be
going too far to describe Frisch as an 'existentialist', despite the
great debt his work so clearly owes to Kierkegaard, his
exploration of the Sartrean notion of individuality and the con-
straints placed upon it by the 'others' and by the 'situation' will
become a central issue in his work, and no more so than in his
most significant drama, *Andorra*. However, before moving on
to a discussion of the play itself, it is essential to trace its earliest
roots in Frisch's imaginative world. For although the play was
first produced in 1961, Frisch's fascination with the theme goes
back to the immediate post-war period.

In 1947 Frisch published a diary-cum-sketchbook, *Tagebuch
mit Marion* which became the opening section of his first major
achievement, the *Tagebuch 1946-1949* (1950). It is in the opening
pages of this extraordinary book, compounded of acute social
and political observation, philosophical speculation and
narrative as well as dramatic fragments, that the short tale, *Der
andorranische Jude*, first made its appearance. This story is the
germ of the play. But before this impressive narrative is looked
at and its relevance to *Andorra* indicated, its own immediate
context must be discussed. For, as Frisch himself warns in his
preface, the fragmentary nature of his *Tagebuch* should not be

taken as an invitation to fragmented reading. Rather, the book
is assembled like a mosaic:

> ... der Leser täte diesem Buch einen großen Gefallen, wenn
> er, nicht nach Laune und Zufall hin und her blätternd, die
> zusammensetzende Folge achtete; die einzelnen Steine
> eines Mosaiks, und als solches ist dieses Buch zumindest
> gewollt, können sich allein kaum verantworten. (II, 349)

The context of *Der andorranische Jude* is indeed a fascinating
one, and one with a dual dimension. Firstly, the story fits into
the 'Marion' complex which follows the (largely emotional)
odyssey of the eponymous hero, a puppeteer in so-called
'Andorran' society. Marion clearly stands for the artist, the
creator and manipulator of images. We first meet him enter-
taining a crowd on a street corner with a puppet, representing
Christ. He is promptly moved on by a policeman, guardian of
law and order, with the self-revealing admonition: 'Das geht
nicht ... Hier nicht ... das geht nicht' (II, 351). The Swiss setting
(the passage is headed 'Zürich, Café de la Terrace') and the
satirical thrust of the incident leave no doubt that the subsequent
passages describing Marion's dealings with the inhabitants of
'Andorra' refer to the author's fellow countrymen. In the
Tagebuch 1946-1949 'Andorra' is unequivocally a metaphor for
Switzerland. Thus the story of the Andorran Jew, in its first
guise, is a story of specifically Swiss mendacity, a warning
against a specifically Swiss brand of hubris. On the broader
level, Marion is a device to demonstrate simultaneously the
enduring fascination of the story represented by his wooden
puppets — Christ, Pontius Pilate, Judas — but at the same time
their loss of vitality. Marion's society is so blind to this dissonance that eventually even Marion himself (as his name hints)
becomes incapable of distinguishing between its members and
his own lifeless marionettes, and he commits suicide. Similarly,
the fate of the Andorran Jew was only possible in a society that
had shut its collective eyes to the enormous implications of the
Nietzschean recognition that God is dead, killed by modern

man's indifference and hypocrisy. In Nietzsche's story[3] it was the madman with his lantern lit at midday who met the incomprehension and mockery of society. Frisch's story takes the Nietzsche parable to its logical conclusion.

The second contextual aspect is to be found in Frisch's discussion of what was to become the dominant theme not just of his *Tagebuch 1946-1949*, but of his whole mature *œuvre*: the secularised exposition of the biblical commandment, 'Du sollst dir kein Bildnis machen'. The human inclination towards making graven images, whether of individuals, entire groups or nations, is declared to be the product of spiritual and emotional lethargy:

> Unsere Meinung, daß wir das andere kennen, ist das Ende der Liebe, jedesmal, aber Ursache und Wirkung liegen vielleicht anders, als wir anzunehmen versucht sind — nicht weil wir das andere kennen, geht unsere Liebe zu Ende, sondern umgekehrt: weil unsere Liebe zu Ende geht, weil ihre Kraft sich erschöpft hat, darum ist der Mensch fertig für uns. Er muß es sein. Wir können nicht mehr! Wir künden ihm die Bereitschaft, auf weitere Verwandlungen einzugehen. Wir verweigern ihm den Anspruch alles Lebendigen, das unfaßbar bleibt, und zugleich sind wir verwundert und enttäuscht, daß unser Verhältnis nicht mehr lebendig sei. (II, 369-70)

Instead of recognising that each individual is an exciting and ultimately unfathomable riddle, a unique entity capable of continual growth, we run out of energy or sympathy: 'Man macht sich ein Bildnis. Das ist das Lieblose, der Verrat' (II, 370). At the same time, Frisch is well aware that we are responsible for each other and for what each of us becomes:

> In gewissem Grad sind wir wirklich das Wesen, das die andern in uns hineinsehen, Freunde wie Feinde. Und umgekehrt! auch wir sind die Verfasser der andern; wir

---

[3] See 'Der tolle Mensch' in *Die fröhliche Wissenschaft* (1882).

sind auf eine heimliche und unentrinnbare Weise
verantwortlich für das Gesicht, das sie uns zeigen,
verantwortlich nicht für ihre Anlage, aber für die
Ausschöpfung dieser Anlage. (II, 371)

There follow directly the story of *Der andorranische Jude* and
Frisch's final lapidary comment:

Du sollst dir kein Bildnis machen, heißt es, von Gott. Es
dürfte auch in diesem Sinne gelten: Gott als das Lebendige
in jedem Menschen, das, was nicht erfaßbar ist. Es ist eine
Versündigung, die wir, so wie sie an uns begangen wird,
fast ohne Unterlaß wieder begehen — Ausgenommen wenn
wir lieben. (II, 374)

The stark position of Sartre, who believed that the Other was
always antagonistic and a threat to autonomy, is clearly softened
in Frisch's meditation on human prejudice. Frisch proclaims
that love, and love alone, can prevent the formation of stulti-
fying images, or at least ensure that the images we perforce have
to make in order to enter into personal relationships remain
flexible and open to constant revision in the light of experience.
It should now be clear that the original story of the Andorran
Jew is embedded in a context vibrant with the humanistic sentiment which is at the heart of Max Frisch's commitment as a
writer.

Der andorranische Jude

In Andorra lebte ein junger Mann, den man für einen Juden hielt. Zu
erzählen wäre die vermeintliche Geschichte seiner Herkunft, sein
täglicher Umgang mit Andorranern, die in ihm den Juden sehen: das
fertige Bildnis, das ihn überall erwartet. Beispielsweise ihr Mißtrauen
gegenüber seinem Gemüt, das ein Jude, wie auch die Andorraner
wissen, nicht haben kann. Er wird auf die Schärfe seines Intellektes
verwiesen, der sich eben dadurch schärft, notgedrungen. Oder sein
Verhältnis zum Geld, das in Andorra auch eine große Rolle spielt: er
wußte, er spürte, was alle wortlos dachten; er prüfte sich, ob es wirklich
so war, daß er stets an das Geld denke, er prüfte sich, bis er entdeckte,

daß es stimmte, es war so, in der Tat, er dachte stets an das Geld. Er gestand es; er stand dazu, und die Andorraner blickten sich an, wortlos, fast ohne ein Zucken der Mundwinkel. Auch in Dingen des Vaterlandes wußte er genau, was sie dachten; sooft er das Wort in den Mund genommen, ließen sie es liegen wie eine Münze, die in den Schmutz gefallen ist. Denn der Jude, auch das wußten die Andorraner, hat Vaterländer, die er wählt, die er kauft, aber nicht ein Vaterland wie wir, nicht ein zugeborenes, und wie wohl er es meinte, wenn es um andorranische Belange ging, er redete in ein Schweigen hinein wie in Watte. Später begriff er, daß es ihm offenbar an Takt fehlte, ja, man sagte es ihm einmal rundheraus, als er, verzagt über ihr Verhalten, geradezu leidenschaftlich wurde. Das Vaterland gehörte den andern, ein für allemal, und daß er es lieben könnte, wurde von ihm nicht erwartet, im Gegenteil, seine beharrlichen Versuche und Werbungen öffneten nur eine Kluft des Verdachtes; er buhlte um eine Gunst, um einen Vorteil, um eine Anbiederung, die man als Mittel zum Zweck empfand auch dann, wenn man selber keinen möglichen Zweck erkannte. So wiederum ging es, bis er eines Tages entdeckte, mit seinem rastlosen und alles zergliedernden Scharfsinn entdeckte, daß er das Vaterland wirklich nicht liebte, schon das bloße Wort nicht, das jedesmal, wenn er es brauchte, ins Peinliche führte. Offenbar hatten sie recht. Offenbar konnte er überhaupt nicht lieben, nicht im andorranischen Sinn; er hatte die Hitze der Leidenschaft, gewiß, dazu die Kälte seines Verstandes, und diesen empfand man als eine immer bereite Geheimwaffe seiner Rachsucht; es fehlte ihm das Gemüt, das Verbindende; es fehlte ihm, und das war unverkennbar, die Wärme des Vertrauens. Der Umgang mit ihm war anregend, ja, aber nicht angenehm, nicht gemütlich. Es gelang ihm nicht, zu sein wie alle andern, und nachdem er es umsonst versucht hatte, nicht aufzufallen, trug er sein Anderssein sogar mit einer Art von Trotz, von Stolz und lauernder Feindschaft dahinter, die er, da sie ihm selber nicht gemütlich war, hinwiederum mit einer geschäftigen Höflichkeit überzuckerte; noch wenn er sich verbeugte, war es eine Art von Vorwurf, als wäre die Umwelt daran schuld, daß er ein Jude ist — Die meisten Andorraner taten ihm nichts.
Also auch nichts Gutes.
Auf der andern Seite gab es auch Andorraner eines freieren und fort-schrittlichen Geistes, wie sie es nannten, eines Gestes, der sich der Menschlichkeit verpflichtet fühlte: sie achteten den Juden, wie sie betonten, gerade um seiner jüdischen Eigenschaften willen, Schärfe des Verstandes und so weiter. Sie standen zu ihm bis zu seinem Tode, der grausam gewesen ist, so grausam und ekelhaft, daß sich auch jene

Andorraner entsetzten, die es nicht berührt hatte, daß schon das ganze Leben grausam war. Das heißt, sie beklagten ihn eigentlich nicht, oder ganz offen gesprochen: sie vermißten ihn nicht — sie empörten sich nur über jene, die ihn getötet hatten, und über die Art, wie das geschehen war, vor allem die Art.
Man redete lange davon.
Bis es sich eines Tages zeigt, was er selber nicht hat wissen können, der Verstorbene: daß er ein Findelkind gewesen, dessen Eltern man später entdeckt hat, ein Andorraner wie unsereiner —
Man redete nicht mehr davon.
Die Andorraner aber, sooft sie in den Spiegel blickten, sahen mit Entsetzen, daß sie selber die Züge des Judas trugen, jeder von ihnen.

What is ostensibly presented as a sketch for a longer narrative, 'Zu erzählen wäre ...', is in fact a superbly crafted, rounded and devastating story. Notwithstanding the specific Switzerland/ Andorra link already established in the opening pages of the *Tagebuch 1946-1949*, the story's structure is that of a parable, that is, the tale's characteristic irony of tone widens the issue to a general statement of man's inhumanity to man. As such it exemplifies with great clarity Frisch's 'Bildnis' theme and in particular the baleful influence the collective can exert on the individual, distorting even his own perception of himself. The function of 'Andorran' image-making is the exact negation of the dialectic which Brecht, for example, analyses in his short essay, *Über das Anfertigen von Bildnissen*.[4] For whilst acknowledging the danger of static images, Brecht saw image-making as a creative interaction between individuals. The question for him was one of avoiding finality and of fashioning images that could point to productive behaviour. For both writers love is crucial as the motivating force between human beings, but Brecht has greater faith in the intellect's ability to guide love to fashion models of positive change for the partner — a faith grounded, of course, in the power and accuracy of Marxist analysis. Frisch, on the other hand, is characteristically more sceptical; he leaves 'love' as an undefined and ultimately mysterious source of energy which once shaped by the conscious

---

[4] 'Notizen zur Philosophie 1929-1941' in: *Schriften zur Politik und Gesellschaft*, *Gesammelte Werke*, Vol. 20 (Frankfurt a.M., Suhrkamp, 1967), pp.168-70.

mind falls inevitably into its opposite: rigidity and fear. Brecht, of course, begs the question of how we are to *know* that any particular 'Bildnis' is good for someone else, whilst Frisch's story is, in part at least, an illustration of the cruel repression that can stem from a society quite secure in its ideological certainties. At the same time, *Der andorranische Jude*, despite its bleak outcome, reveals a flash of optimism which links it to Brecht's Marxist parables: the Andorrans *are* shown to be capable of recognising their guilt, indeed the recognition engenders an undiluted and inescapable horror. What we have here is an apparently intact belief in the efficacy of the moralising parable. The suggestion is that self-awareness is possible and man therefore corrigible. It is, in fact, the noble belief that fired Lessing and underpinned the whole Enlightenment tradition. Furthermore, the didactic impact on the characters within the tale is clearly expected to be matched by that on the reader, whether in Switzerland/Andorra or elsewhere. In other words, Frisch's story exhibits a relatively unshaken confidence in the power of literature to convey moral imperatives — a confidence, ironically enough, which the later pages of the *Tagebuch 1946-1949* themselves progressively undermine, and which is markedly missing from the dramatic explorations of human blindness and stupidity in the plays leading up to *Andorra*, such as *Die Chinesische Mauer* (1947/55), *Graf Öderland* (1951), *Don Juan oder Die Liebe zur Geometrie* (1953), and in particular *Biedermann und die Brandstifter* (1958) with its wry subtitle 'Ein Lehrstück ohne Lehre'.

In *Der andorranische Jude*, however, language and message are fused into a single powerful unit. Frisch is magnificently in control of his method and material: subtle shifts of tone; a deceptively flat narrative style; the depth-charge placing of the only 'wir' in the narrative which implicates the reader almost without his noticing the fact until it is too late; the equally telling use of 'man' which starts in relaxed neutrality and culminates in a panic flight into the would-be safety of anonymity. All these features will reappear in the later play transformed into dramatic rhythm and gesture.

Interestingly, the decision to dramatise *Der andorranische*

Jude was not the result of an impulse or a sudden insight into the suitability of the material, but evolved slowly from a series of public readings Frisch gave of the sketch. That is to say, the dialectic between performer and audience gradually made Frisch realise that this theme was not only a major dramatic one, but somehow peculiarly *his* theme: 'Gerade darum zögerte ich lang, wissend, daß man nicht jedes Jahr seinen Stoff findet', he admitted in an interview with Horst Bienek (*2*, p.32). Ironically, it is to this hesitation that we owe Frisch's other major theatrical success, *Biedermann und die Brandstifter*, which he undertook firstly for urgent financial reasons, but secondly as a necessary 'Fingerübung' before tackling *Andorra* itself (*2*, p.32). He eventually began work on the latter in 1958 (IV, 579). Indeed, the play was originally destined for the 1958/59 season as part of the Zurich Schauspielhaus's jubilee celebrations. However, the material proved unexpectedly intractable. In all, Frisch wrote the play five times, its title changing from *Zeit für Andorra*, via *Modell Andorra* to the final simplicity Frisch settled on in January 1961. Premièred in that year on 2nd, 3rd and 4th November — the three evenings were necessary to accommodate the extraordinary critical interest at home and abroad — the play was promptly seen as a significant contribution to the burgeoning phenomenon of what was termed 'Bewältigungs-literatur', that is, the attempt by German poets, novelists and dramatists to come to terms with the problems of Germany's recent past. For example, Heinrich Böll's novels, *Billard um halb zehn* (1958) and *Ansichten eines Clowns* (1961), the first two parts of Günter Grass's 'Danzig Trilogy', *Die Blechtrommel* (1959) and *Katz und Maus* (1961), together with the widely popular *Diary of Anne Frank* (1956) and the now forgotten Erwin Sylvanus's *Korczak und die Kinder* (1957), not to mention Sartre's *Les Séquestrés d'Altona* (1959), which received its German première in Munich in April 1960, all helped to provide a ready framework into which *Andorra* appeared neatly to fit. But to see the play thus exclusively in the context of 'Holocaust' literature is to misunderstand its true meaning. For the theme of *Andorra* is both more complex — and ultimately more uncomfortable.

As we have seen, the origins of the play are not to be located in the atmosphere of the late 1950s, but in Frisch's response to the immediate post-war period — the response, that is, of a perplexed intellectual freed from the problematical comfort of neutrality and forced to face the criminal enormity of a fascist régime whose leading representatives were products of a civilisation to which he himself, through language and culture, was intimately and inextricably related. The story of the Andorran Jew (despite its undoubted Swiss dimension) is linked directly to the theme of *Nun singen sie wieder*: Frisch believes that we are all capable of the moral blindness and narrowness of spirit which characterised the Third Reich or, to be more accurate, there is no guarantee that we too, faced with a similar situation, would not behave like the vast majority of ordinary people, who, whilst personally avoiding bestiality, allowed it both to happen and flourish in their midst.

This belief was by no means an isolated one in post-war Switzerland. It was most cogently argued by Max Picard in his controversial book, *Hitler in uns selbst* (1946). Like Frisch, Picard was fascinated by the nature of human evil and was concerned above all to combat the instinctive desire to demonise it (and thus relativise its specifically human roots) or, more crudely, to consider its most recent eruption as a phenomenon peculiar to German society under Hitler. Picard's central thesis was that, given the general fragmentation of culture and the increasing tendency of modern civilisation towards abstraction and away from the immediate and concrete, we are all prone to the same disease that struck Weimar Germany and culminated in National Socialism. (Indeed, it had already infected that latently anti-Semitic segment of the Swiss bourgeoisie that had created the fascist National Front.[5])

Whilst Frisch did not share Picard's ahistorical, Christian standpoint, he certainly matched his compatriot's concern to

---

[5] See Alfred A. Häsler, *Das Boot ist voll...Die Schweiz und die Flüchtlinge 1933-45* (Zurich, Ex Libris, 1967) and Walter Wolf, *Faschismus in der Schweiz: die Geschichte der Frontenbewegung in der deutschen Schweiz* (Zurich, Flamberg, 1969). For a study of Swiss anti-Semitism in the nineteenth century, see Friedrich Külling, *Bei uns wie überall? Antisemitismus* (Zurich, Juris, no date).

resist the temptation to condemn Germany out of hand and thus avoid the necessity for critical self-reflection. To this extent at least, Frisch's theme can be said to fit into a growing anti-Swiss polemic which reached a peak in his novel *Stiller* (1954) and which has continued unabated with *Wilhelm Tell für die Schule* (1971), which seeks with mordant wit to dismantle the national myth, with the harsh strictures of his revised memoirs of military service, *Dienstbüchlein* (1974), and with numerous speeches and political interventions since. Frisch's emphasis on the dangers of creating graven images thus forms both an admonition of those fellow countrymen who exhibited a smug sense of superiority in the face of a powerful and arrogant neighbour laid low, and at the same time a generalised statement about human, as opposed to merely 'Swiss' or 'German', behaviour patterns.

The most striking change in the transposition of the brief anecdote to the full dimension of the theatre is the shift from the individual, 'der andorranische Jude' to the collective, 'Andorra'. Gone is the admirable, but naive post-war belief in love as a mysterious power protecting men and women from their debilitating inadequacies; the theme is now unequivocally the destructive nature of prejudice, both on its victim (Andri) *and* on its perpetrators (the Andorrans). At the root of the play is an uncompromising dissection of the neuroses that underpin false attitudes, that help to sustain false identities. The problem of identity, indeed, has long been recognised as Frisch's personal obsession, and in *Andorra* it receives particularly stringent attention. The Classical concept of personality, embodied most powerfully in the German tradition by Goethe's view of individual potential as something realised in an organic process of creative evolution, nourished by the social, intellectual and emotional environment, has proved to be a noble, but ultimately unconvincing ideal in the twentieth century where socio-economic and political pressures, far from encouraging a unique sense of identity, have in fact been the agent of immense distortions. Thus in *Andorra*, Frisch uses anti-Semitism as a telling paradigm for the corrupting influence that a dislocated and dishonest society can exert upon its members. The search for identity undertaken by the individual is shown to be vitiated and distorted by the majority, locked in a system of fear and anxiety, which presents itself ironically as a coherent group held together by an unshakeable confidence in its own sense of belonging.

The second major change in the metamorphosis from narrative to drama is the addition of a completely new and intricate family tragedy. The full import of this extension, its weaknesses and strengths, must be left for later analysis, but the central point here is that the story of Can, his relationship with the Señora and his children, is exemplary in the same way as the theme of anti-Semitism. For this 'private' tragedy set against the 'public' dissonance serves to highlight precisely the infernal nature of the mechanism set in train when men and women forsake their true selves in favour of an inauthentic existence. Indeed, in a profound sense, Can falls greater victim to the latter than any of the other Andorrans he so heartily despises.

This then is the picture Frisch paints of his model Andorra, whose very name suggests that barrenness of spirit (dorr/dürr = barren) which creates victims, designates fellow human beings as hapless outsiders and needs the despised Other ('Andri') to disguise its own sense of inadequacy. In Frisch's hands, anti-Semitism, the most virulent and destructive negativity in our Christian culture, is merely the most frightening example of human intolerance in recent history. This is not to belittle the immense tragedy of the Holocaust or to relativise and thus trivialise the suffering of Central European Jewry; indeed, the fact that Andri is *not* a Jew is essential to a correct understanding of Frisch's theme. For the removal of even this disgraceful rationale from the Andorrans' defensive stance reveals with even greater clarity the irrational source of their imbalance. By this paradoxical twist, Frisch is able to trace more vividly in the play than in the narrative mode the *mechanics* of prejudice. The aim of the play is to show how attitudes are formed and deformed, and the catastrophic effects these can have both on the persecuted and the persecutors themselves.

In this connection, it is important to stress the fact that Frisch's Andorra is deliberately presented more in terms of a peasant or at least agrarian community than in those of the

highly industrialised mass society of the early twentieth century
which spawned fascism. This is certainly not a failure on the part
of the dramatist to get to grips with the socio-economic forces
that were crucial to the success of National Socialism in
Germany. Critics who labour this point forget that they are
dealing not with an academic treatise, but with the theatre and
the abstractions of art. But even if such a socio-economic
analysis were possible in terms of effective drama, which is
doubtful, this is emphatically not Frisch's purpose in writing
Andorra. The model he chooses to present is that of a close
community, where personal ties are tangible and where everyone
knows everyone else. Andorra, in other words, is the place we
would like to live in, sometimes convince ourselves we still do;
the fake village invented by city-dwellers to counter their sense
of uprootedness. To use the terms of the German sociologist
Ferdinand Tönnies, Andorra is the organic 'Gemeinschaft'
opposed to the impersonality of the modern 'Gesellschaft'. This
is not ahistorical on Frisch's part, for his model intends to reveal
dishonesty in all its guises. And the Andorran belief that they
live in a unique, coherent and stable communion is clearly the
most powerful myth that obscures the true nature of their
reality. In this vaguely idyllic 'Gemeinschaft' (familiar to us all,
but even more so to the Swiss where the social units are smaller
and more closely-knit) a common pride and a common sense of
direction apparently underpin their Andorran identity. It is an
essential part of Frisch's purpose to expose this myth for what it
is: a network of subterfuge, bad faith and half-truths. His
model, suitably abstracted for greater impact, reveals the notion
of an intact and authentic society as a peculiarly dangerous
illusion.

Frisch's dissection of 'Andorran' anti-Semitism, indeed, fits
very closely the analysis published in 1944 by Jean-Paul Sartre in
his essay *Réflexions sur la question juive*.[6] Andri's non-
Jewishness exemplifies Sartre's uncompromising assertion in
that book: 'Le juif est un homme que les autres hommes
tiennent pour un juif' (p.83f). Indeed, Frisch's argument

[6] *Réflexions sur la question juive* [1944] (Paris, Gallimard, 1954).

matches Sartre's exactly: 'L'anti-sémitisme n'est pas de problème juif: c'est *notre* problème' (p.184). For as Sartre demonstrates, we *all* contribute to the 'situation' in which the Jew, the Outsider, the scapegoat of whatever kind, finds himself. Andorra in this light is not simply a vision of Switzerland, but the arid, negative areas of our own minds in which it is so comfortable to rest and forget the strains and stresses created by full and open contact with other human beings.

If this were not the case, Frisch would indeed be guilty of creating a grotesque graven image of his own country and its people, as some — especially Swiss! — critics have maintained. Karl Schmid, for example, in his influential study *Unbehagen im Kleinstaat* (1963) devoted a whole chapter, entitled 'Max Frisch: Andorra und die Entscheidung', to a careful examination of this question. His analysis of Frisch's frequently bitter attitude towards Switzerland deserves special attention not only for its quality, but also for his unusual sensitivity towards Frisch's predicament as a non-conformist intellectual in a country which prizes conformity as the highest civic virtue. Schmid discusses the idea that Switzerland was not forced to take an unambiguous stand towards fascism simply because its historical principle of neutrality and its peculiar geographical position — 'eine vergraste Provinz abseits der Geschichte' to quote Albin Zollinger[7] — never exposed it to such evil temptation, and suggests that this idea led Frisch to create an absurd caricature of the Helvetic Confederation.

Whilst this criticism possesses some plausibility within the overall context of the other writers Schmid discusses — Conrad Ferdinand Meyer, Henri-Frédéric Amiel, Jacob Schaffner and Jacob Burckhardt — it does not convince when crudely applied to *Andorra*. It is true that Frisch's relationship with his fellow countrymen has been, and continues to be, far from harmonious — a fact well known to Karl Schmid (see the warm exchange of letters between the two men printed in later editions of Schmid's book). And certainly at times Frisch — not a man of placid

---

[7] Albin Zollinger, *Pfannenstiel* [1940], *Gesammelte Werke*, Vol. 3 (Zurich, Atlantis, 1962), p.252.

temperament — has been provoked by petty animosities and wilful misunderstandings into utterances that come very close to the sentiments of the Lehrer Can; for example, when he remarked in an interview with the Austrian writer Gerhard Roth in 1981:

> Misanthropisch sehe ich nur die eigenen Leute, die Deutschschweizer. Das ist wahr, daß ich diese Brut nicht leiden kann, natürlich, weil man diese Züge auch selber hat, das ist verbunden mit einem gewissen Selbstekel. (*3*, p.28)

But a differentiation has to be made between the creative work and the overtly political controversies in which Frisch, the stubborn and often reluctant native of Zurich, has frequently been involved.

In the case of *Andorra*, the rebuttal of Schmid's thesis can be made on two grounds. Firstly, it is a time-honoured method in didactic theatre to pare down a complex social reality in order to reveal more clearly the bones and structure of that reality. At an extreme but everyday level it is, of course, the technique of the political cartoonist. Secondly, in so far as the play refers specifically to Switzerland at all, it is not about what that country *did*, but what under certain pressures it *might* have done. Yet the potential for 'Andorran' behaviour is clearly not bound to one nationality, as the sad history of the last twenty-five years has amply demonstrated. If the Swiss feel uniquely attacked in *Andorra*, then that has less to do with Frisch's animus than with the fact that neutral Switzerland's undisturbed progress through the cataclysmic upheavals of the twentieth century has enabled the Swiss, more than most, to cling to the Pharisaic belief that they are still the active representatives of the pioneering achievements of nineteenth-century liberalism.

Frisch's purpose then is more ambitious than to construct a straightforward satire on Swiss sanctimoniousness and hypocrisy. He wants us to see *Andorra* with his other plays as:

> ... keine Zeitstücke im landläufigen Sinn. Es sind immer

wiederkehrende Muster, tragische Muster ... Mich interessiert der Beginn einer Katastrophe. Wann ist der Punkt des Neinsagens? Wenn man die Katastrophe erkennt, ist es meist viel zu spät. Das Schlimmste ist, sich daran zu gewöhnen. (*40*, p.19)

Andorra, Frisch wrote to George Tabori in October 1962, 'ist nicht eine allegorische Illustration der Geschichte, sondern greift hinter die Geschichte' (*40*, p.19). Thus, notwithstanding the fact that *Andorra* can be seen at one level as an attempted demonstration of the complacent image the Swiss have of themselves, its wider implications cannot be ignored. As Frisch put it in the programme note for the Zurich première:

Gemeint ist natürlich nicht der wirkliche Kleinstaat dieses Namens, nicht das Völklein in den Pyrenäen, das ich nicht kenne, auch nicht ein anderer wirklicher Kleinstaat, den ich kenne; Andorra ist der Name für ein Modell. Es gibt ja noch eine andere Weltkarte; auf ihr, und nirgends sonst, finden wir das Illyrien von Shakespeare, das Güllen von Dürrenmatt, das Sezuan von Brecht, das Troja von Giraudoux usw. (reprinted in *55*, p.41)

Over a decade later in a speech accepting the 1974 Großer Schillerpreis of the Swiss Schiller Foundation, Frisch reiterated the point succinctly, if with a slightly different emphasis: '*Andorra* ist nicht die Schweiz, nur das Modell einer Angst, es könnte die Schweiz sein; Angst eines Schweizers offenbar' (VI, 514). And that surely is the key to *Andorra*.

2. Structure

Andorra is a model, that is a small-scale version of reality, an abstraction which enables us to perceive the contours and structures of that reality without the danger of getting bogged down in naturalistic detail. At the same time, it is a model of a different kind: it is a sketch of an imagined world against which we can test the reality *outside* the theatre (*40*, p.72). Because *Andorra* is in a sense an exploration rather than an obvious piece of didacticism in the manner of Brecht's *Lehrstücke*, it succeeds in being more open-ended, and it is this very open-endedness that differentiates Frisch's use of the parable form from that of Brecht. The latter's mature concept of theatre was of course underpinned by his faith in Marxist ideology. His study of Marx convinced Brecht that the twin 'sciences' of economics and sociology could penetrate and illuminate the obscure workings of the capitalist world. Since there was nothing static about this world, it logically followed that once recognised, it could be changed by the alteration of the prevailing economic conditions. Furthermore this change was not only desirable, but actually inevitable, since the dominant structures would sooner or later collapse beneath the weight of their own inherent contradictions. Man, too, was part of this dialectical process and subject to the same dynamic change as the institutions he had created. In other words, Brecht — the true heir to the Enlightenment tradition — believed that man and society could and should be changed for the better. And one agent of this desirable process was the theatre. Man was educable; he could learn from the communal demonstration of his situation, suitably transformed or 'alienated' by a scientific theatrical method. The famous 'Verfremdungseffekt' was the central technique in showing what appears to the senses as static and familiar in a new dynamic light that would provoke the spectator into thinking critically and perceiving the necessity for, and the right course of, action.

Against this optimistic didacticism Frisch remained profoundly sceptical. Moralising on the stage, offering through an
aesthetically congruent form obvious instructions on how to
think, did not match his experience of the theatre nor did it
appear to influence the world in general. Indeed, he explicitly
rejected the possibility of such certain effects in an early entry in
his *Tagebuch 1946-1949*, in which he castigates what he calls 'die
andorranische Kunst unsrer Tage', which is characterised by the
aesthetic pretence that the old 'classical' values are still intact,
untouched by two world wars and the progressive dehuman-
isation of twentieth-century technology:

> So könnte es Zeiten geben, wo nur noch Stümper sich an
> die Vollendung wagen. Noch ist es nicht soweit. Ein
> Katholik beispielsweise, der sich in einer geschlossenen
> Ordnung glauben kann, hat natürlich die Erlaubnis zur
> Vollendung; seine Welt ist vollendet. Die Haltung der
> meisten Zeitgenossen aber, glaube ich, ist die Frage, und
> ihre Form, solange eine ganze Antwort fehlt, kann nur
> vorläufig sein; für sie ist vielleicht das einzige Gesicht, das
> sich mit Anstand tragen läßt, wirklich das Fragment.
>
> (II, 451)

In the spirit of this diary entry, the parable *Andorra* does not
show a clear set of moral alternatives in classical form, but poses
a worrying question mark concerning the individual
responsibility of each and everyone of us. This question is raised
insistently at each level of the play whose circularity of form, by
its very viciousness, paradoxically mocks the neatly rounded
conclusions preferred by the mentally lazy. *Andorra* offers the
spectator no easy escape into the comfortable routines of
ideology. And yet, if Frisch now promises himself no radical
social improvement via the medium of literature, nor from the
performance of his play in the theatre, he nevertheless retains a
belief in the possibility, remote but persistent, that individual
consciousness at least might be modified by exposure to its
critical paradoxes (*1*, p.38).

The play is constructed in two distinct halves: scenes 1-6 deal with the ways the Andorrans fix a false identity onto Andri, the supposed Jewish foundling, whilst scenes 7-12 illustrate the disastrous impact of such attitudes on the human freedom of the individual who is exposed to them. The dialectic between truth and lie unites the two halves in a complex but highly ironic whole. Finally the interpolated scenes at the witness stand link past to present and, acting as an 'epic' commentary on past events, these episodes hold the key to the play's meaning.

In accord with Frisch's strategy of inviting the audience to identify with the Andorrans, or at least initially to tolerate their apparently harmless idiosyncrasies, before distancing themselves when it is far too late (*Anmerkungen zu 'Andorra'*, IV, 561), the play opens on a light, festive note. In a masterly piece of exposition Barblin is seen engaged in the traditional white-washing of her parents' house. But against her naïveté and innocence and Father Benedict's projection of an idyllic community, 'ein schneeweißes Andorra' (IV, 414), is immediately set the sexual crudity of the soldier, Peider. His unpleasantly sarcastic attitude towards the venerable customs of the country he is paid to defend unwittingly points to the dubious nature of this community and anticipates its ultimate collapse:

> Wenn bloß kein Platzregen kommt über Nacht! Nämlich seine Kirche ist nicht so weiß, wie sie tut, das hat sich herausgestellt, nämlich seine Kirche ist auch nur aus Erde gemacht, und die Erde ist rot, und wenn ein Platzregen kommt, das saut euch jedesmal die Tünche herab, als hätte man eine Sau darauf geschlachtet ... (IV, 465)

With such skilful economy of means Frisch establishes the atmosphere of a lull before a storm, an atmosphere in which the Priest's engaging simplicities are offset by the incipient disharmony exhibited by the other Andorrans. Typically the truth, embodied in Peider's words, comes from a tainted source and is therefore not recognised: Andorra's 'purity' is ensured not by any spiritual renewal, but by the expedient covering up of reality by gestures emptied of moral significance.

The first half of the play amply illustrates this fundamental lack of integrity, as each Andorran in turn is depicted treating Andri with varying degrees of dishonesty. Now twenty years old, the Jewish foundling is about to claim his rightful place in the community, demanding from his fellow citizens a more concrete commitment than the self-congratulatory tolerance which Andri as a child has inspired. Slowly but surely Andri's modest, and significantly typical Andorran aspirations, coupled with the increasing pressure from the fascist Blacks on Andorra's borders, arouse in the Andorran population their latent anti-Semitism. In scene after scene the Soldier, the Innkeeper, the Carpenter, the Doctor and the Apprentice modify their attitudes to produce a dramatic rhythm which thrusts Andri ever deeper into the labyrinth of a false identity. Each gesture, in itself relatively harmless, increases the pressure which denies Andri the chance to be himself. The graven image first created by his father Can is gladly accepted by the Andorrans as the ready-made excuse for their own prejudiced behaviour.

The first six scenes of *Andorra* are thus characterised by the ubiquitous lie, set in motion by the Teacher, Can, for obscure reasons which we will have to examine later. Its insidious impact upon his son is like the tightening threads of a spider's web as they locate the potential victim. What began as a structure of interlocking relationships providing the individual with a sense of place and security is now revealed as a murderous trap. The second half of the play illustrates the increasingly desperate struggles of the protagonist as his freedom of movement is progressively curtailed. Indeed, it is fundamental to the play's humanist message to grasp the significance and nature of this struggle, that is, Andri's peculiar response to the pressures exerted upon him. In the first half of the play he is presented as an entirely conformist individual, his ambitions as circumscribed as Andorra itself. The sudden rejection by his community acts almost like a curse: 'ich habe meinen Namen in die Lüfte geworfen wie eine Mütze, die niemand gehört wenn nicht mir, und herunter fällt ein Stein, der mich tötet' (IV, 527). In this poignant image is summed up the two dramatic movements in the play: an outburst of innocent joy and hope is

crushed by the soulless aridity at which the name Andorra itself
hints. The stone that crushes the life out of Andri (as it does his
mother) is fashioned in all its evil rigidity in scenes 7-12. The
damage has already been done: these final scenes are therefore
given over to Andri's stubborn, almost pathological, defence of
an essentially spurious identity. The paradox is bitter: the more
Andri 'feels' he is a Jew, the more plainly he becomes an
Andorran. It is the fascinating demonstration of the fatal effect
of such dislocated behaviour that points to *Andorra* being
substantially more than a relatively uncomplicated contribution
to that body of post-war German literature which attempted to
come to terms with the fascist past. If this had been the case, the
Jew-inspection scene could have immediately followed scene 6.
The play would have been over (see *55*, p.309f). Instead Frisch
develops his graven image theme to its logical and infinitely
more appalling conclusion.

The Jew inspection, in fact, is the culmination of a dual
dramatic movement: the projection of an inauthentic existence
onto a scapegoat and the scapegoat's acceptance of that false
identity. Criticised by some as an incongruous change of style,
the scene is, on the contrary, a coherent summation of Frisch's
central theme, its abstraction an intensification of the model's
own structure. Nevertheless, its staging requires extremely
careful handling. François Bondy, among others, remarked on
the embarrassed reaction to the scene at the Zurich première
when the director, Kurt Hirschfeld, allowed it to degenerate
from the macabre to the grotesque (*47*, p.60). The key to the
scene lies in its sharply *visual* quality, underlined by the fact that
the invading Blacks and their Jew Inspector never utter a single
word. Instead their presence can be seen as the embodiment of
Andorran speech. These mute invaders are simply the outward
manifestation of the Andorrans' own corrupt mental attitudes.
They are therefore properly anonymous, symbolically black and
devastatingly silent. Frisch made his intention with this difficult
scene particularly clear in his letter to George Tabori, already
mentioned:

Die Judenschau (eine Erfindung, eine freie Erfindung, um

so unheimlicher, je weniger sie an historische Fakten
erinnert) ist 'mystisch', mittelalterlich wie der Antisemitismus überhaupt, legendär; der Zuschauer soll das
Gefühl haben und hat es auch, das sei ein Brauch, den nur
er nicht kennt. (*55*, p.60)

It is for this reason that Frisch did not wish the Blacks to be
either demonic or reminiscent of any historical evil, precisely in
order to reveal their unacknowledged origins in the very banality
of Andorran everyday life. Thus the Jew Inspector is infallible in
his selections not because of some mysterious biological sixth
sense, but because the 'Jew' has already been adequately marked
out by the Andorrans themselves. As Frisch wrote in a letter to
his publishers: 'Für mich ... gehört es zum Wesentlichen des
Einfalls, daß die Andorraner ihren Jud nicht töten, sie machen
ihn nur zum Jud in einer Welt, wo das ein Todesurteil ist' (*55*,
p.53). As the Andorrans' identity is obliterated by the black
cloths they are forced to pull over their heads and their voices
become muffled and indistinguishable from each other, the Jew
inspection turns into a chilling reminder that social attitudes are
encapsulated in a common language and that such language can
prove lethal. Far from being a *Stilbruch*, the scene is an
impressive illustration of George Büchner's similarly frightening
vision in his play *Dantons Tod*. There Büchner has Mercier say
bitterly to his fellow Dantonists in Act III, scene 3: 'Geht einmal
euren Phrasen nach, bis zu dem Punkt wo sie verkörpert
werden. Blickt um euch, das Alles habt ihr gesprochen, es ist
eine mimische Übersetzung eurer Worte.'
    The efficient speed of the Jew Inspector's methods (admired
significantly by the Doctor, the least secure of the Andorrans)
mocks in a peculiarly painful way the haphazard, disorganised
and initially harmless-seeming anti-Semitism exhibited by the
Andorrans in the first half of the play. Sweating with fear, the
Andorrans are left to cope with their own mendacity. This they
do by the time-honoured method of transferring their sense of
horror and guilt from the major issue to the minor, from the
death of Andri to the barbarity of the ring torn from his finger:
'Das mit dem Finger ging zu weit ...' (IV, 557). Hypocrisy is the

great trivialiser; drink will soon complete the anaesthetisation of such delicate sensibilities.

The final image of Barblin, crazed and shorn of her hair, indicates the truth that often it is only the mad who can see clearly. The festive white-washing of the opening scene has now revealed its full symbolic significance: 'Ich weißle, ich weißle, auf daß wir ein weißes Andorra haben, ihr Mörder, ein schnee-weißes Andorra, ich weißle euch alle — alle' (IV, 558). This recurring motif effectively underlines the play's attack on Andorran duplicity, for it sums up the vicious circularity of guilt and repression from which the Andorrans are incapable of breaking free. The circle is indeed closed on a bleak note of universal cowardice and failure: 'Ich möchte keinen Hoffnungsstrahl am Ende, ich möchte vielmehr mit dem Schrei enden, wie skandalös Menschen mit Menschen umgehen' (Frisch in an interview with Curt Riess, *49*).

The most important structural element in *Andorra*, however, is one which Frisch ironically settled on only in his final draft and worked out in rehearsal: the interpolated scenes at the witness stand (see *55*, pp.29ff, 163). As Frisch himself has acknowledged (*1*, p.26), this 'epic' material owes a great deal to Brecht's influence. These short scenes serve to distance the main action by placing it in the *past*. The point is crucial to a proper understanding of the play, for it demonstrates with absolute clarity that the Andorrans, far from undergoing a process of enlightenment, have not yet even begun to ponder the nature of their behaviour and responsibility. The flashback technique, familiar enough to any film-goer, underscores the Andorrans' incorrigibility: the passage of time has brought no evaluation of their role nor any insight into their own motivation. The decision made at rehearsal, to have the Andorrans at a witness stand placed parallel to the stalls rather than confronting them, both establishes the quasi-judicial atmosphere and ensures that the audience cannot escape into the role of judge. For as Frisch remarked in the Riess interview (*49*):

Die Schuldigen sitzen im Parkett. Sie, die sagen, daß sie es nicht gewollt haben. Sie, die schuldig wurden, sich aber nicht schuldig fühlen. Sie sollen erschrecken, sie sollen, wenn sie das Stück gesehen haben, nachts wachliegen. Die Mitschuldigen sind überall.

The mirror image of the original story, in which each individual privately saw his own guilty reflection, is to be transformed, as befits the theatre, into a *communal* experience. The difference, of course, is that the dramatist does not have sovereign control over his audience's perception. What he can declare to be fact in the story, he can only hope to achieve in the drama. How far Frisch succeeded in his aim I will try to assess when I examine the play's reception.

Technically the scenes at the witness stand effectively unite the two time levels, past and present, in a dialectic which gives the play its proper perspective: the emphasis is unequivocally on the *here and now.* On the one hand, their 'epic' nature helps to remove the traditional suspense of the conventional, naturalistic theatre, that is, they shift attention in a Brechtian manner from *what* will happen to *how* it will do so, from *whether* Andri will die to *how* his death comes about; on the other hand, these short scenes do not conform entirely to Brecht's theory of the 'Verfremdungseffekt', for they do not in fact break the illusion in order to distance the audience for the purposes of critical reflection. The information they convey and the perspective they create generate the peculiar dramatic tension which holds the whole play together. Whilst they make clear the tragic outcome of the story unfolding before us, they arouse our curiosity about the true role of each individual in the affair:

Wirt: Hab ich ihn vielleicht an den Pfahl gebracht?
(IV, 477)
Tischler: Ich bin nicht schuld, daß es so gekommen ist
später. (IV, 481)
Geselle: Ich bin nicht schuld, daß sie ihn geholt haben
später. (IV, 487)
Soldat: Aber ich habe ihn nicht getötet. Ich habe nur
meinen Dienst getan. (IV, 503)
Pater: ... auch ich habe ihn gefesselt, auch ich habe ihn

an den Pfahl gebracht. (IV, 509)
Jemand: Was die Soldaten, als sie ihn holten, gemacht
        haben mit ihm, weiß ich nicht, wir hörten nur
        seinen Schrei... (IV, 529)
Doktor: Eine tragische Geschichte, kein Zweifel. Ich bin
        nicht schuld, daß es dazu gekommen ist. (IV, 542)

The odd thing about their statements is that though the
Andorrans (with the exception of the Priest) are ostensibly
witnesses, giving evidence before an unspecified tribunal, all
their energy is absorbed in protesting their own innocence. Their
words, as much as their unchanged circumstances (only the
Apprentice and the Soldier appear to have changed their
previous roles, and significantly *their* 'evidence' reveals the most
undisguised prejudice) stress the continuity of Andorran society
and the attitudes which sustain it. It is the audience, not Frisch's
characters, which is to undergo what the Andorrans refuse: a
cathartic recognition. For this to have its full impact it is
essential that Frisch draw the audience into the Andorrans'
guilty conspiracy, or at least prevent it from rejecting their
moral shiftiness too prematurely. What these skilfully
interpolated scenes demonstrate, of course, is that in 1961 (and
one could as easily write 1985) *nothing has changed*. The moral
ambiguities, the evasive ambivalence reassert their baleful
dominance as the play's dramatic rhythm drives to its
preordained conclusion.

3. Characters

Perhaps the most striking feature of *Andorra* is Frisch's differentiated handling of character. On the one hand, the Andorrans are put forward as types in harmony with the essential nature of the parable form; on the other, three characters — Can, Barblin and Andri himself, that is the Family — are singled out for more rounded treatment. It is this fact that has led critics to note the peculiarly mixed dramatic form Frisch has created (see Hans Wysling, 55, p.133), and indeed, the psychological intensity of the family dimension which Frisch has added to the original story strongly recalls the central theme of Ibsen's theatre. As far as the 'everyday' Andorrans are concerned (Peider, Prader, Ferrer, Fedri, Father Benedict, the Doctor, the Somebody), these are clearly reduced to their functions in this society rather than portrayed as complex individuals. They are thus closely related to the earlier theatrical methods of German Expressionism. Frisch, however, explicitly warns against turning these characters into caricatures (IV, 561). All art is a form of abstraction, and it is important that any director of *Andorra* should find the gesture and rhythm for these types that will enable Frisch's parabolic shorthand to illumine social reality rather than obscure it. For these particular roles, despite superficial resemblances, are not truly Expressionist in their conception, but are more akin to the typology of the more ancient tradition of the morality play, which was of course also a source of inspiration for the Expressionists.

The Andorrans are thus meant to reveal general human attitudes whilst representing individual aspects of a collective one. The realistic quality of their puppet-like behaviour paradoxically offsets the more fully sketched humanity of the Family. In this the technique, as has been frequently noted, is strongly reminiscent of Büchner's *Woyzeck* (see, for example,

Armin Arnold, *18*, pp.297-311). In that play, the unique quality
of Marie and Woyzeck is similarly underlined by the automaton
behaviour of the social types surrounding them. They too are
dramatically alive because they suffer in quite individual ways,
whereas the representatives of their society are shown to be
morally blinkered, sad reductions of their true selves, like the
Andorrans in Frisch's play.

Nevertheless, the argument could be raised that Frisch, by
reducing his Andorrans to their social functions and yet
expecting us to respond to them — at least initially — with
empathy, is guilty of creating the very graven images of human
reality that he is at such pains to castigate as the most insidious
danger to human relationships. Such a criticism, however, stems
from a basic confusion between art and life. Frisch's strictures
relate specifically to real life outside the theatre; what *Andorra*
represents is a model to help us understand, and thus be better
placed to come to terms with, that complex reality. The theatre,
in other words, is a kind of neutral space in which ideas,
ideology, are illuminated, tested and continually modified. The
central paradox of drama is that a fixed text is kept fluid, not
merely by individual directors' vision and the actors'
performance, but also — and most importantly — by the
dialectical interaction with a constantly changing audience.
Those critics who maintain the simplistic attitude that 'Andorra'
is, say, Switzerland and the 'Blacks' are the Nazis are themselves
guilty of creating graven images, not Max Frisch.

Of course, Frisch recognises that 'Bildnisse' are an inevitable
concomitant of our human thought-processes, that our attitudes
and beliefs are inevitably coloured, even distorted, by ideology
which 'hat die Tendenz, sich zu verfestigen, zu versteinern,
unwirklich zu werden, sich von der Wirklichkeit zu lösen', but
the aim of the theatre, as of all art, is to refuse to succumb to
this depressing process and to exert its power against it: 'Die
Ideologie muß also auch immer wieder gesprengt werden' (*1*,
p.48). It is a peculiar instance of intellectual blindness to see
Andorra, in this sense, as a self-defeating contribution to the
very propensity it sets out to attack. The role of literature for
Frisch — and his play is no exception — is:

die Ideologie zu verunsichern, indem sie immer wieder versucht, die sich verändernde Realität ins Bild zu bringen, zur Darstellung zu bringen; und da zeigt sich dann die Diskrepanz zwischen dem Vokabular der Ideologie und der mit ihr verbundenen Realität. Daher ist die Literatur ... immer ein subversives Unternehmen ... ein therapeutisches Unternehmen. (*1*, p.48)

Accordingly, the 'Bildnisse' Frisch creates in *Andorra* are not those he alluded to in his *Tagebuch 1946-1949*, but closer to Brecht's more positive formulation in *Über das Anfertigen von Bildnissen*: 'Kleine Modelle, die ... verraten, wie sie funktionieren.'[8] The aim then is to create abstractions (models) from observed reality which will help to unmask the mechanisms of human behaviour — in *Andorra* the nature of individual and collective prejudice. The Andorrans are dramatised aspects of a coherent whole, their dramatic function pared down for greater didactic effect.

Before I discuss these types individually — for despite the economy of their realisation, they each have a distinct personality within their overall one-dimensionality — the family at the centre of this web of dishonesty requires a full analysis. For the tragedy of Can and the Señora (the Mother needs no special comment) encapsulates both the ingrained mendacity and the moral corruption of Andorran society.

THE FAMILY

It cannot be denied that the addition of this 'private' dimension to the original sketch in the *Tagebuch 1946-1949* caused Frisch immense dramaturgical problems, not all of which have been satisfactorily solved. However, the decision to illustrate the far-reaching violence of prejudice by showing its impact on society's smallest and most crucial unit was entirely justified if the play was to avoid the pitfall of political sloganising. Traditionally, of course, the family should provide that haven of love and order within which every human being

---

[8] *Gesammelte Werke*, Vol. 20, p.168.

can grow and achieve his or her full potential. Can's family is the very reverse: it is rooted in deceit, hypocrisy and a wilful arrogance which hides its rotten core. In a word, it is *Andorran*.

Can

In a letter to Carl Zuckmayer, dated 15 July 1961 (*MFA*), Frisch admitted that Can was always 'eine blöde Crux', in that his motivation was exceedingly difficult to dramatise. Why and how did this erstwhile brave 'Eber' (IV, 488), who tore up school textbooks rather than teach the lies they contained (an interesting sidelight on Andorran society even before the threat of invasion from their Black neighbours!), turn into this morose alcoholic who has lied for twenty years about the true origins of his own son? Zuckmayer felt that the banal motive of wishing to avoid an unpleasant confrontation with his wife might have been a better option. But this would surely have been a trivialisation, and fortunately Frisch chose the more difficult course of attempting the sobering portrayal of a man whose independence of mind and moral strength have been fatally undermined by a moment's aberration. The decision to hide Andri's true parentage is clearly in part — as the Señora points out — a welcome opportunity to disguise a personal dishonesty behind a mask of apparent bravery, and pass himself off as the intrepid defender of the weak and vulnerable — the Jewish foundling — against the brutality of the Black's pogrom. To assuage his conscience, however, he has convinced himself that his true motive is to teach his fellow Andorrans in due course a harsh lesson: 'Sie werden sich wundern, wenn ich die Wahrheit sage. Ich werde dieses Volk vor seinen Spiegel zwingen, sein Lachen wird ihm gefrieren' (IV, 469). The Teacher, desperately trying to identify with his self-imposed mission of political and moral enlightenment is forced to recognise that his dubious strategem, neatly convincing at the time, has taken on a momentum of its own. The lie is not a harmless didactic weapon waiting to be used, but a lived reality which can only corrupt truth: 'Einmal werd ich die Wahrheit sagen — das meint man, aber die Lüge ist ein Egel, sie hat die Wahrheit ausgesaugt. Das wächst. Ich werd's nimmer los' (IV, 497). It is the insidious growth of the lie's tentacles that effectively prevents Can from telling Andri the truth when the revelation has become a matter of life and death. Twenty years of dissimulation cannot be shaken off in a moment. The unexpected threat of incest, posed by the love of Andri and Barblin, paralyses an already weakened will.

Hans Bänziger was the first to point to the similarity between Can's predicament and that of Lessing's father-figure in *Nathan der Weise* (5, p.111). The danger of incest between unwitting brother and sister in the earlier play is, however, easily obviated by the power of reason and tolerance to influence the mind; Lessing re-establishes the true nature of the family in a triumphal eighteenth-century vision of universal brotherhood. But this restatement of primal innocence and order is not an option given to a dramatist in the second half of the twentieth century, where chance has replaced divine providence. Can's would-be didacticism, unlike Nathan's, is deeply vitiated by his own dishonesty. As his wife remarks with undisguised bitterness: 'Du hast uns alle verraten, aber den Andri vor allem. Fluch nicht auf die Andorraner, du selbst bist einer' (IV, 523). By the time he has faced up to the truth that his behaviour two decades ago was, in fact, rooted in *fear* of his own kind, not in a misguided didacticism — 'Ein Andorraner, sagen sie, hat nichts mit einer von drüben und schon gar nicht ein Kind. Ich hatte Angst vor ihnen, ja, Angst vor Andorra, weil ich feig war ... Es war leichter, damals, ein Judenkind zu haben. Es war rühmlich' (IV, 533) — it is far too late. His son cannot and will not believe him. His forlorn attempt to play the role of the just man founders on his own contradictory nature.

The key to the human fascination of Can's character — and the play is *his* tragedy as much as it is his son's — lies precisely in this mixture of strength and weakness. His suffering, expressed in his deeply ironic inarticulateness, lends him a pathos matched only in the characterisation of Andri. This 'unique' Andorran is brought to realise that his proud independence and his elitist scorn for Andorran prejudices are a brittle fiction, a false identity as much as Andri's Jewishness. His Judas-like self-punishment, after he has seen the full extent of his false role-playing and its effect, ensures that he is absent from the witness

stand when the other Andorrans seek to justify *their* roles, but
merely emphasises his flawed humanity.

The Señora

The role of the Señora was sharply curtailed as Frisch worked
on the final draft of the play. In fact, the interpolated witness
stand scenes replaced a series of episodes in which excerpts from
the letters exchanged between Can and his mistress were to be
read (see *55*, p.29). The story of their affair was consequently
reduced to a single confrontation placed between scenes 8 and 9.

It cannot be said that Frisch found the ideal solution for this
dramaturgical problem. On the one hand, he was surely right to
decide against extending the private dimension to include the
early history of Can and the Señora; on the other, the character
has now become so tenuous as to border on the implausible. The
Señora's rediscovery of maternal instinct after twenty years is
left quite unexplained, and her curious agreement (IV, 521) not
to tell Andri the truth herself looks suspiciously like a clumsy
theatrical device.

Nevertheless, there are moments in her last conversation with
Andri (scene 9) when the character suggests depth. In particular,
her sad reflection on the disappointed hopes of her own youth
have the ring of truth and help to throw some light on her
relationship with Can:

> Als ich in deinem Alter war: mein Vater, ein Offizier, war
> gefallen im Krieg, ich weiß, wie er dachte, und ich wollte
> nicht denken wie er. Wir wollten eine andere Welt. Wir
> waren jung wie du, und was man uns lehrte, war
> mörderisch, das wußten wir. Und wir verachteten die Welt,
> wie sie ist, wir durchschauten sie und wollten eine andere
> wagen. Und wir wagten sie auch. Wir wollten keine Angst
> haben vor den Leuten. Um nichts in der Welt. Wir wollten
> nicht lügen. Als wir sahen, daß wir die Angst nur ver-
> schwiegen, haßten wir einander. Unsere andere Welt
> dauerte nicht lang ... Kein Mensch, wenn er die Welt sieht,
> die sie ihm hinterlassen, versteht seine Eltern. (IV, 522)

Transience and loss of energy, cowardice and fear, mark the human condition in the land of the Blacks as it does in Andorra. The pressures of the collective on the rebellious individual are patently the same. But one speech does not make a character, and the Señora's presence in the play is determined ultimately more by structural requirements than by thematic coherence.

Barblin

Not all critics would grant that Barblin is a fully rounded character; many see her as a weak echo of those familiar dramatic archetypes, Goethe's Gretchen and Shakespeare's Ophelia. It is true that Barblin's fate, her unhappy love and collapse into insanity, has a number of powerful antecedents in the theatre, but her capacity for suffering effectively sets her apart from the other Andorrans. Although Barblin does not have the puzzled, painful incoherence of Büchner's Marie in *Woyzeck* (with whom she is frequently compared), her confusion as she succumbs to the intolerable pressure within Andorra does come across in the hands of a sensitive actress. Nevertheless, the motivation of her character — in particular her relationship with Peider which is the final irreversible betrayal in Andri's mind — caused Frisch considerable difficulties as he admitted to Zuckmayer in the letter quoted earlier and recorded in his rehearsal notes ('Der Schrei', IV, 563-65). The problem lies in her essential passivity. As she only responds to events and — with the sole exception of the attempt to incite resistance against the Blacks' orders — never initiates them, she plays a peripheral role; yet she is a character who remains oddly in the mind. In particular, as the individual who with her whitewashing *gestus* links both the first and final scenes of the play, she acquires a tragic dignity which raises her above the trite. Her final gesture of placing Andri's shoes to await his return is one of the most evocative and powerful moments in the play: 'Hier sind seine Schuh. Rührt sie nicht an! Wenn er wiederkommt, das hier sind seine Schuh' (IV, 560). These poignant words remind us that it was Barblin who first uttered the word 'Jude' in the play. The voice of loving concern therefore is given not only the single most important word to introduce, and one which progressively becomes distorted in the Andorrans' mouths, but she is also given the last gesture to underline that emotion which, as we have seen, is the only one which Frisch believes can save us from creating our deadly images of each other.

Andri

In the letter to George Tabori, the translator of the version for New York, Frisch declared that it was essential that Andri should not be played as a 'Musterknabe. Er soll uns auch manchmal schockieren wie jeder andere Mensch' (55, p.57). And indeed, our first experience of Andri is a recognition of his basic ordinariness. His youthful exuberance, limited mental horizons, distinguish him in no way from the rest of the Andorrans. He shares their self-satisfied conviction that Andorra is the centre of the universe; his ambitions — job, marriage to the girl next door, peer-group acceptance — are thoroughly unexceptional. Perhaps his only idiosyncratic feature, compared at least with the adult world around him, is his insouciant attitude towards money which he happily wastes on the juke-box. In other words, Andri's first scenes serve to establish his naive perception of his environment as a peaceful idyll in which a comfortable niche is guaranteed for him too.

His status as archetypal victim, however, is immediately plain to the audience by Frisch placing the first witness stand scene directly after the opening scene. There the Innkeeper washes his hands of Andri's fate 'nach Jahr und Tag' (IV, 477). It is this dual perspective which creates the tension and fascination of the Andri role. The more we see him attempting to claim his Andorran birthright — or, from his point of view, the rights of any individual in this 'Hort der Freiheit' — the more we the audience are made aware that he is unwittingly being driven deeper and deeper into a quagmire of prejudice from which there will be no escape. As we have seen, the first half of the play consists of the gradual disabusement of Andri. The paradox is that the more he is rejected by the community in which he has been brought up, the more he appears to take on quite specific Andorran characteristics. It is here that *Andorra* comes closest to the traditional morality play; for the Andorrans each exhibit one or more of the seven deadly sins of biblical tradition and proceed to project these onto their chosen 'Sündenbock' as alien 'Jewish' defects: pride, covetousness, greed, lechery, envy, anger and sloth. Indeed, Frisch's play is a perfect illustration of the analysis of anti-Semitism produced by Max Horkheimer and Theodor Adorno in their study, *Dialectic of Enlightenment*: 'The portrait of the Jews that the nationalists offer the world is in fact their own self-portrait.'[9] Thus the Innkeeper is covetous, the Carpenter greedy, the Soldier lecherous, the Doctor envious, the Teacher angry, the Priest spiritually slothful; and all, even perversely Can himself, are inordinately proud of their national distinctiveness and innate moral superiority. In other words, Andri becomes a convenient target onto which they can focus their own secret weaknesses and fears and so be rid of the pressures such personal failings generate.

The result of such social pressures is to deform the individual to whom they are applied, and the second half of the play demonstrates this process in terms of Andri's character. From the moment of his ostensible betrayal by Barblin, Andri assumes and tries to defend with a perverse obduracy the false identity that the others have fashioned for him. In an attenuated form the Andorrans' sins become his, their fundamental mendacity becomes his reality. The individual is divorced from the roots of his own identity. There is indeed a characteristic Andorran element in Andri's rigid responses to Father Benedict at the play's psychological climax in scene 9. The word 'Wahrheit' which runs as a leitmotif throughout this impressive scene is progressively emptied of meaning. Andri, fatally confused by the Andorrans' relativisation of the concept, flees into his false role: 'Euch hab ich ausgeglaubt' (IV, 526). Betrayed by his father whose drunkenness thwarts his last minute attempt to put right a twenty-year-old wrong, deceived, as he thinks, by Barblin, Andri bitterly embraces his 'Jewishness' and in his turn condemns his father and scorns his sister. The disruption of the family is total. Andri's loss of his true self is dramatically highlighted by his devastating reply to the shocked Priest:

[9] *Dialectic of Enlightenment* [1944] (London, Allen Lane, 1973), p.168.

Ich möchte nicht Vater noch Mutter haben, damit ihr Tod
nicht über mich komme mit Schmerz und Verzweiflung
und mein Tod nicht über sie. Und keine Schwester und
keine Braut: Bald wird alles zerrissen, da hilft kein Schwur
und nicht unsre Treue. Ich möchte, daß es bald geschehe.
Ich bin alt. ... Meine Trauer erhebt mich über euch alle,
und so werde ich stürzen. Meine Augen sind groß von
Schwermut, mein Blut weiß alles, und ich möchte tot sein.
Aber mir graut vor dem Sterben. Es gibt keine Gnade —
                                                                    (IV, 527)

The strong Old Testament echoes and rhythms of this extraordinary speech — Frisch wrote the monologue not as conscious
pastiche, but from his memory of Jewish tradition (see *40*, p.64)
— underscore the isolation and acute dislocation of Andri's
mind. Thrust out of the community, he has no choice but to
deny his father and mother. He is locked in a vicious circle of
fear, anger and mendacity; he can therefore only grasp the
Andorran lie as his reality and *become* the Andorran Jew (see
55, p.152). In a devastating reply to Can he makes this entirely
plain: 'Ich weiß, wer meine Vorfahren sind. Tausende und
Hunderttausende sind gestorben am Pfahl, ihr Schicksal ist mein
Schicksal' (IV, 534). Thus Andri's tragic development is an
exemplary illustration of Frisch's 'Bildnis' theory: inherent in
the creation of graven images are inchoate dangers and
unpredictable violence; for the process not only destroys the
victim, but utterly perverts the humanity of the perpetrators too.

THE ANDORRANS

The basic human vices represented in the characters of the
Innkeeper, Carpenter, Apprentice, Soldier, Priest, the
Somebody and the Doctor have already been touched on. What
gives this typology its greater resonance is the retrospective cast
of the play; for our view of the individual Andorrans becomes
progressively coloured by their contemporary attitudes towards
their common past which they reveal at the witness stand.
Because the play's structure enables us to receive the two time

levels simultaneously, we cannot — unlike the Andorrans — escape into the comfortable vagueness of a defective memory. Rather are we forced to do what the 'witnesses' so singularly fail to do: think critically about the past and its relationship to the present.

Peider

Nowhere is this refusal to think critically better exemplified than in the bully and braggart, Peider the Soldier. Hiding his cowardice behind his uniform, Peider stands for all those soldiers whose motivation for joining the army is to escape all responsibility for shaping their own lives. Not without a certain intelligence — after all, he at least has seen through the Church's irrelevance in Andorra! — Peider pursues his gross appetites whilst giving full rein to his prejudices. The word 'Jew' becomes in his mouth a dehumanising label to be attached to any convenient outsider as a means of bolstering up his own insecure ego. The man who boasts that Andorrans will fight for their integrity 'bis zum letzten Mann' becomes without any psychological progression the willing tool of the invading oppressor. It is therefore highly fitting that it is *his* voice which is dominant in the Jew inspection and the preliminary announcements. The Blacks will always find such quislings to do their work for them, individuals whose belief that 'Order ist Order' represents an ever-open escape hatch for their conscience.

Despite or because of the one-dimensionality of this character, the Soldier is a timely and chilling reminder that all absolute power depends on obscure individuals to translate its oppression into reality. Peider's defence, years later in civilian life, is typically revealing. Alone among the Andorrans he feels secure enough to reassert his anti-Semitism: 'Übrigens glaube ich noch heute, daß er einer gewesen ist. Ich hab ihn nicht leiden können von Anfang an' (IV, 503). He is transfixed in a smug sense of having done his duty, of having obeyed orders, for 'Wo kämen wir hin, wenn Befehle nicht ausgeführt werden!' (IV, 503). For Peider the past has no relevance to the present. And yet his deliberate avoidance of the word 'Jud', never far from his lips in his army days, points to his shabby dissembling.

The Innkeeper

The Innkeeper is the first witness to appear at the witness stand, and fittingly so, for it is he who in the play's opening scene appears as the most harmless in his prejudices. Like the others, however, he marks out Andri as different — but initially employs him as an exception, 'eine regelrechte Ausnahme', of course, who will not harm trade. His prompt exploitation of Can's need to raise money for Andri's apprenticeship is to a certain extent softened by his apparent willingness to criticise his own people (and by implication his own actions): 'Natürlich ist's Wucher! Die Andorraner sind gemütliche Leut, aber wenn es ums Geld geht ... dann sind sie wie der Jud' (IV, 469). However, even this self-deprecating attempt at humour immediately assumes a sinister note when he appears in the very next scene at the witness stand to deny his guilt 'nach Jahr und Tag': 'Hab ich ihn vielleicht an den Pfahl gebracht? Niemand von uns hat wissen können, daß Andri wirklich sein eigner Sohn ist, der Sohn von unsrem Lehrer ... Ich bin nicht schuld' (IV, 477). The rhythm of his words condemns him unequivocally. The implication that the 'error' was not the murder, but the mistaken identity, is clear to all but the speaker. That the Innkeeper should also be the one who killed the Señora — his panic-stricken behaviour at the Jew inspection contrasts sharply with his smooth avowal at the witness stand — is the final comment on this species of bourgeois harmlessness, the man whose fragmentary conscience causes a telling linguistic slip when he excitedly declares his willingness to defend his country: 'Ich wäre der erste, der einen Stein wirft' (IV, 512).

The Carpenter

The Carpenter too has learnt nothing from the past. Like his colleague the Innkeeper, his evidence consists of unwittingly confirming his own ingrained anti-Semitism: 'Wieso wollte er nicht Verkäufer werden? Ich dachte, das würd ihm liegen' (IV, 481). Once again mistaken identity is seen as the real problem. Resentment and vicious prejudice still lurk just below the surface. The only weak point in his behaviour 'damals' — the extortionate demand for fifty pounds as the fee for an apprenticeship — is now explained as a stratagem to keep Andri out of the workshop to avoid unpleasantness with his other employees. The Carpenter's conscience has clearly lost nothing of its customary elasticity.

The Apprentice

The minor figure of the Apprentice takes his share of the general cowardice. His fear for his own position prevents him from owning up to the shoddy workmanship which is 'naturally' blamed on Andri, and thus his overtures of friendship are revealed as the hollow gesture that they are. Although he admits his fault at the witness stand, he still manages to shift the blame onto the victim: Andri's anger at the injustice is taken as full justification for the Apprentince's attitude. Once again the juxtaposition of his past behaviour and his current desire to defend himself bears eloquent testimony to the contradictions of his personality: 'Nachher hab ich ihn *auch* nicht mehr leiden können, geb ich zu' (my emphasis) is followed by 'Als wir ihn nochmals fragten wegen Fußball, da war er sich schon zu gut für uns' (IV, 487). This Apprentice has not only learnt all the tricks of his trade, but with his ability to channel resentment into wounded innocence, he has in the meantime clearly become a fully qualified member of Andorran society.

The Somebody

Of all the Andorrans, the Somebody ('Jemand'), as befits his name, is both the shadowiest and the most ubiquitous. In some ways he is also the most sinister. Stripped even of a social function, he represents the archetypal 'Mitläufer', the cynical fellow-traveller whose survival depends entirely on his skill of adapting to the prevailing power structure. He is acutely aware of the shifts in atmosphere — 'Ein schwüler Abend, ich glaub, es hängt ein Gewitter in der Luft' (IV, 467) — and is thus able to adjust with great rapidity. Mischievously, Frisch presents him as something of an intellectual with a neat turn of phrase. He is also equipped with a cynical sense of humour which enables him to keep his distance from the other Andorrans. Indeed, he calls himself at one point with a characteristic sneer 'ein fröhlicher Charakter' (IV, 513), and his reluctance to identify himself any further enables him to seem omnipresent despite the relatively little text he is given. Yet by the Jew inspection he is indistinguishable from his compatriots, despite his superior air and wit. The character is in fact the embodiment of moral relativism: trimming and adapting is his second nature. Always on the periphery of affairs, watchfully waiting to see the advantageous way to jump, his secret lies in his ability to present a façade of balanced reasonableness to the world. 'Ich möchte niemand beschuldigen, ich bin nicht der Weltenrichter' (IV, 529), he declares in his brief statement at the witness stand. For, of course, if no one can be accused, he too can escape all opprobrium. The success of his survival strategy is linked to society accepting his highly attractive proposition: 'Einmal muß man auch vergessen können, finde ich' (IV, 529).

The Doctor

The Doctor is the only Andorran who seizes the chance for a lengthy self-defence at the witness stand, which he introduces with the false modesty of 'Ich möchte mich kurz fassen ...' He is, of course, the Andorran with the greatest sense of personal resentment which he projects on to the Jew, the virulent monster of his imagination, who has both prevented his professional advancement and forced him to return a failure to the provincial backwater of his native country. His bitterness and frustration take the form of an exaggerated praise for Andorra, 'ein Hort des Friedens und der Freiheit und der Menschenrechte' (IV, 511). Loquacious and bigoted, he is incapable of sticking to a coherent pattern of prejudice: at one moment the Jews have apparently prevented him from achieving his deserved professorship, the next he has given up 'alle Lehrstühle der Welt' (IV, 510) in order to return to his beloved country. Such threadbare dishonesty and naked anti-Semitism prepare us well for his appearance at the witness stand. There all the characteristic Andorran traits are plainly revealed: the truculence, the defensive and highly characteristic shift from 'ich' to 'wir', the defective memory — all geared to self-exculpation. His speech is a masterpiece of dissembling self-justification. Although he claims to know a good deal which could correct contemporary misapprehensions, where personal guilt might be suspected, his memory fails him or he takes refuge either in the abstract pronoun 'man' or the first person plural. The false regrets, the pseudo-historical perspective, the cheap sentiment are brilliantly articulated by Frisch as the Doctor's fertile brain is made to spawn thought processes whose very rhythms betray the thoughts the words are designed to obscure:

> Ich bestreite keineswegs, daß wir sozusagen einer gewissen Aktualität erlegen sind. Es war, vergessen wir nicht, eine aufgeregte Zeit ... Eine tragische Geschichte, kein Zweifel. Ich bin nicht schuld, daß es dazu gekommen ist. Ich glaube im Namen aller zu sprechen, wenn ich, um zum Schluß zu kommen, nochmals wiederhole, daß wir den Lauf der Dinge — damals — nur bedauern können. (IV, 542)

Thus is language used ironically to unmask reprehensible, indeed catastrophic attitudes which remain as deeply ingrained in current Andorran society as they were in the troubled past.

Significantly, it is the Doctor who unwittingly gives the whole game away when at the beginning of the very next flashback (the Jew inspection) he is made to say:

> Nur keine Aufregung. Wenn die Judenschau vorbei ist, bleibt alles wie bisher. Kein Andorraner hat etwas zu fürchten, das haben wir schwarz auf weiß. Ich bleibe Amtsarzt, und der Wirt bleibt Wirt, Andorra bleibt andorranisch ... (IV, 543)

In a letter to Fritz Kortner, dated 2 March 1962 (*MFA*), Frisch himself delcared that the Doctor's anti-Semitism was the really dangerous brand of that evil, precisely because it was expressed so 'elegantly'. It is this man's perverted intelligence, in other words, which can convince weaker intellects that efficiency is an absolute virtue ('Wie sie einem ganzen Volk diese Tücher verteilen: ohne ein lautes Wort! Das nenne ich Organisation. Seht euch das an! Wie das klappt', IV, 544).

Black is white if it works. Of all the Andorrans, the Doctor is the most ready to abdicate his critical faculties in order to save his skin. Neither education nor foreign travel has broadened his mind; they have merely consolidated an incorrigible arrogance. The ability to forget, or at most remember selectively, is his guarantee of continued office. He is Frisch's foremost example of that dismal twentieth-century phenomenon, 'la trahison des clercs'.

The Priest

Apart from Can, Father Benedict is the only other guilty Andorran who does not appear at the witness stand. However, whereas the Teacher has drawn the logical conclusion from his Judas role and hanged himself, there is no such escape for the Priest. The one man who could have saved Andri in that he knows both his real identity and that he could not have been responsible for the Señora's murder, is astonishingly and conspicuously absent from the Jew inspection. Though, unlike the others, he does now recognise his part in Andri's tragedy — indeed, he is given the crucial biblical text to utter — Father Benedict can apparently still see no way of translating his insight into practical action. He has taken the first, fundamental step, but his confession remains restricted to the privacy of his own church — a secret between himself and his God. In this way Frisch points to the moral ambiguity of an institution within a society whose behaviour patterns it patently shares.

The Priest is in many ways the crucial figure in Andorran society. He stands above the others precisely because *in the context* he represents 'ein möglichst anständiger Christ; nur so hat sein Versagen das historische Format', as Frisch remarked in the letter to Fritz Kortner, quoted above. Indeed, in this character Frisch has realised a most insidious type of anti-Semitism — that which masquerades (often unknown to the conscious mind) as a progressive *philo*semitism. Father Benedict singles Andri out — just like the others — but in his case for approbation 'grad weil du anders bist als alle' (IV, 506). But here too the well-meaning Priest is given away by the inadvertent phrases which momentarily, but crucially, disturb the smooth flow of rhetoric: 'Weißt du, Andri, was du bist? ... Ein

Prachtskerl! In deiner Art. Ein Prachtskerl!' (IV, 505). The qualifying 'in deiner Art' is the clue to the Priest's real feelings that his 'professional' Christianity can barely hide. Later, his deep-rooted prejudice comes blatantly to the surface in a moment of intense irritation: 'Ich habe dir gesagt, Andri, als Christ, daß ich dich liebe — aber eine Unart, das muß ich leider schon sagen, habt ihr alle' (IV, 507). The typical note of Andorran ambivalence is clear even in this man of God: the Jew should conform to 'Christian' standards of 'love', the Jew's obdurate over-sensibility creates endless difficulties for the magnanimous and the tolerant. The scene in which this exchange takes place (scene 7) significantly opens the second half of the play, and it ends with a gestus of great symbolic impact. The Priest's bad faith is rendered palpable by the altar boy who helps him silently to dress for Mass. As each garment is laid upon him — properly, evocative reminders of Christ's passion — Father Benedict becomes more rigid and inhuman, his language more cliché-ridden: ''s ein Funke in euch. Denk an Einstein! Und wie sie alle heißen. Spinoza!' (IV, 508). Even the tell-tale elision — not normally a feature of this educated man's speech — relates him to the Andorra of the Innkeeper and the Carpenter.

The dichotomy between language and meaning, so vividly caught in this scene, is intensified in the final encounter between the two men which forms the play's psychological climax. Charged with telling Andri the truth of his birth against the backcloth of rising public agitation, the surrogate father can only repeat the disastrous failing of Andri's biological father, Can. The changes Father Benedict urges Andri to acknowledge, the latter can only see as momentary and minor deviations from an all too well understood pattern of behaviour. The truth, as often happens in Frisch's work, comes from such a tainted source that it forfeits all power to achieve good. Far from 'redeeming' Andri — the sinful pride of the Priest's formulation is revealing — Father Benedict merely succeeds in driving the hapless victim further into his false identity. As Andri remarks percipiently: 'Alle benehmen sich heut wie Marionetten, wenn die Fäden durcheinander sind, auch Sie, Hochwürden' (IV, 524).

Together with the Teacher, the Priest belongs to that category of 'progressive' Andorrans mentioned in the original prose sketch. Their particular contribution to this grim catalogue of guilt has to be properly recognised if Frisch's intention is to be fully achieved, that is, to uncover 'die kleinen und scheinbar noch harmlosen Ansätze, die ersten Risse in der Mauer; das bedenkenlose Mitmachertum, die Feigheit, lange bevor Widerstand nur noch für Märtyrer-Typen in Frage kommt' (55, p.19).

4. Language

In the fullest account of Frisch's language to date, Walter Schenker records that in writing *Andorra* Frisch saw his task as one of inventing a form of dialogue which would enable the spectator to feel: 'So sprechen die Leute in Andorra, sie sprechen nicht wie aus einem Buch, sondern wie Einheimische' (*26*, p.31). Frisch has been outstandingly successful in this critical area of the play, and his success stems from his skilful exploitation of the tensions that have always existed for him between his native *Mundart* and *Hochdeutsch*, the standard written form of the language. That the specific *Mundart* informing the tone and rhythms of Andorran speech is clearly that of the author's native country is both unavoidable and its particular strength. But this should not be taken as 'proof' that Andorra is, after all, Switzerland; for though it is undeniable that the dialogue has an especially sharp resonance for the Swiss, it is sufficiently stylised to generalise its applicability. The dialect colouring — deliberate Helveticisms are not employed — helps to intensify the aura of authenticity the language conveys.

Accordingly, the Andorrans' speech reveals the typically abbreviated patterns of Alemannic German: 'Jud', 'drum', 'ist's', 'hierzuland', 'sehn', 'die Schuh' — elisions which for instance are not present in the Señora's speech since she is a foreigner. Interestingly, the Doctor, as an educated Andorran with much experience ouside his native country, avoids the too obvious cadences of his native land at those moments — at the Jew inspection and, in particular, at the witness stand — when he feels his superior diction could be of some advantage to him. The effect is to create a loose and fluently colloquial language which is both convincing and eminently actable. It allows within its typifying features a good measure of differentiation. The crudities of Peider, for example, can be accommodated as well as the smug rhetoric of the Doctor, the mellifluous sententiousness of the Priest and the guilty irrascibility of Can. Yet all are immediately recognisable as members of the same linguistic group.

An intelligent analysis of Andorran speech patterns has characterised it as a 'Rollensprache' (*40*, p.56); and in the sense that the Andorrans use language in a mindless, uncritical manner, preferring the comfort of cliché and slogan to the effort of original thought — 'ein schneeweißes Andorra', 'lieber tot als Untertan', 'ein Stuhl von Prader ist ein Stuhl von Prader', 'der Andorraner ist nüchtern und schlicht', 'der Andorraner macht keine Bücklinge', 'kein Mensch kann aus seiner Haut heraus', 'unsere Waffe ist unsere Unschuld' — this is an accurate description of their mental laziness and secondhand living. Fused with their one-dimensional roles, their dialogues are variations on a fundamental solipsism that their speeches at the witness stand merely underline. They are not individuals in charge of their own speech, but puppets who are moved by linguistic strings fashioned by collective fears and prejudices. Unwittingly, they reveal with words of self-praise and self-exculpation their own moral turpitude: language and intention are disastrously out of phase.

Frisch's demonstration of how language escapes conscious control to achieve a quasi-autonomy which deforms personality is seen not only in the evasive cadences of the Andorrans at the witness stand, but at its most intense in scene 9 where Father Benedict confronts a desperate Andri. Andri's language at that point, as we have seen, marks the total internalisation of the false identity which has been so comprehensively prepared for him: he no longer speaks as a naive, happy-go-lucky young man, but in the painful rhythms reminiscent of the Old Testament. The fact that the images chosen are those of archetypal Jewish suffering merely underscores Andri's loss of individuality, the violence this society has done to his true self. As Frühwald and Schmitz point out, the syntax of Andri's great speech reveals the structures of a stylised Yiddish, the effect of which demonstrates 'die Isolation des Sprechenden und macht das Selbstbild transparent' (*40*, p.61). The bitter irony of Andri's tragedy is that he dies in order to keep intact the lie he has come firmly to believe in.

Biblical language, however, is not just echoed in this crucial scene; it forms the resonant background to all Andorran speech. Indeed, there are constant quotations or overt references to the Bible throughout the play: 'Weißelt ihr Jungfrauen, weißelt' (IV, 464; cp. Psalm 51), 'Kindermord zu Bethlehem' (IV, 465; cp. Matthew 2. 16-18), 'Ich bin nicht schuld' (IV, 477, 481, 542; cp. Matthew 27. 24), 'lobpreiset eure Zedern vom Libanon' (IV, 483; Psalm 92), 'Sintflut von Milch' (IV, 498; cp. Genesis 7. 10), 'Du sollst dir kein Bildnis machen' (IV, 509; cp. Exodus 20. 4), the triple stage direction 'Hahne krähen' (IV, 501; cp. Matthew 26. 34 and 74, Luke 22. 34 and 60-61, John 13. 38 and 18. 27), 'die Letzten werden die Ersten sein' (IV, 510; cp. Matthew 19. 30), 'Ich wäre der erste, der einen Stein wirft' (IV, 512; cp. John 8. 7), 'Wo hast du die Schleuder, David?' (IV, 516; cp. I Samuel 17. 49-50), 'Warum küssen Sie mich?' (IV, 522; cp. Luke 22. 48), 'Sündenbock' (IV, 533; cp. Leviticus 16. 21-22), 'Wo hast du meinen Bruder hingebracht?' (IV, 559; cp. Genesis 4). These references naturally serve in the first instance to characterise Andorran society as conservative and still in contact, however tenuously, with its historic cultural roots (see *40*, p.63). But their combined effect, especially in the cases where the reference or quotation is inaccurate or only half-remembered, is to intensify further the exemplary nature of Frisch's parable play. The ancient story of Cain and Abel, and the Passion of Christ are once more re-enacted in the framework of a secularised model which deprives the victim and his fate of all relevance to the traditional redemptive pattern. Man's inhumanity to man is Frisch's theme, not the illustration of any metaphysical argument. The fragments of tradition that cling to *his* story merely highlight that tradition's comprehensive collapse.

In his dialogue Frisch was thus concerned to create a specific 'Sprachklima' (*40*, p.64); for only by this means could he effectively illustrate the fatal divorce between meaning and language, character and thought, that is characteristic of Andorran society — today as much as 'yesterday'. The stronger their apparent belief in the clichés they utter, the plainer it becomes to the audience that the fabric of a once vital faith has disintegrated, leaving a rigid insensitivity and a moral emptiness.

Frisch's use of Christian imagery in this sense reveals once more his debt to the early German Expressionists, for example, Ernst Toller and Georg Kaiser, who also exploited the peculiar tensions of religious vocabulary in an age which had declared the death of God.

Such stylisation, of course, is inevitable in any theatrical performance. On the stage all language is an abstraction from its natural form outside the theatre. The skill lies in creating a synthesis of style and naturalistic speech. This Frisch has admirably achieved in *Andorra*. Apart from the biblical allusions discussed above, the dialogue contains some powerful symbolism. The most obvious example is the white/black antithesis which runs throughout the play — and in particular linking the first and last scenes. Purity and cleanliness is the symbolic aim of Barblin's traditional whitewashing of her father's house on the eve of St George's Day; at the end the symbolic action has darkened into a feverish attempt to whitewash the *whole* of Andorra where innocent blood has left an ineradicable stain, but one visible only to the deranged. The 'schneeweißes Andorra' has become as black as the uniforms of the ominously silent invader, the Andorrans' faces are white, not with innocence but with fear and terror, as they are blotted out under the black cloths.

Shoes, too, play a poignant role in Frisch's handling of symbol. A clear echo of the sad piles of clothing left behind by the victims of Nazi concentration camps, Andri's randomly discarded shoes are the final image of desolation and horror in the play. But above all it is the invisible 'Pfahl' which reverberates most distinctly in the play. Seen only by the Teacher, its existence is merely verbal — a suggestion made in rehearsal by Kurt Hirschfeld — but by transplanting this central image with its echo of the Cross into our imaginations, its full symbolic power is realised. The more the Andorrans refuse to 'see' this projection of their own minds, the more the audience is able to perceive its murderous reality.

The witness stand has already been discussed, but its relationship to language also needs comment. Its physcial isolation — Frisch indicates no other paraphernalia which might indicate a courtroom — infuses the object with symbolic significance.

Clearly this is no normal, secular court with victim and accused, nor is their relationship to be ascertained by a well-established process of law. The Andorrans are instead merely 'witnesses' to their own behaviour and their own past; they stand at the bar of their own conscience and, one after another, miss the last opportunity to locate and recognise the truth.

The virtuosity of language which Frisch displays in *Andorra* is the play's greatest strength. Its flexibility and subtlety ensure that the parable is not reduced to a specific time and place. If the play has lost its fascination for the contemporary theatre, this is due not to the inadequacies of its language, but to the fact that we have grown indifferent to parables with such an insistently humanistic message.

5. Reception

If *Andorra* represents Max Frisch's most ambitious drama, it also has proved to be his most contentious one. Despite the huge impact of the Zurich première and the play's subsequent triumphal progress through West Germany, it evoked from the very beginning an ambivalent response from both theatre-goers and academic critics which cast a curious light on its commercial success. The two principal areas of contention were on the one hand the problem of conflicting theatrical styles (produced mainly by the attempt to fuse 'private' and 'public' thematic material), and on the other, the fundamental concept of the play as a 'model'.

In the course of my discussion of the main aspects of the play, I touched on a number of weaknesses which stem largely from the addition of the 'Ibsenish' family tragedy to the original 'Brechtian' story published in the *Tagebuch 1946-1949*. The formal problems this involved were effectively summed up by Hans Wysling when he isolated not just two, but five different dramatic modes operating in the play: 'Das epische Theater (Brecht), das analytische Drama (Ibsen), das idealistische Drama in sozio-psychologischer Modernisierung, das Märtyrerdrama, die antike Tragödie' (*55*, p.133). His conclusion was distinctly provocative:

> Der *dramaturgische Synkretismus* enthüllt die Ratlosigkeit eines modernen Autors, der sich über die Instanzen, von denen die Geschicke der Individuen und Gruppen gelenkt werden könnten, nicht mehr im klaren ist. (*55*, p.136)

However, whether the family conflict and the typical 'Frischian' identity crisis, which afflicts (and ultimately helps to destroy) Andri, detract from or intensify the central issue which the model aims to illuminate, is perhaps after all a question which

can only be answered satisfactorily by each individual confronting the text in the theatre itself. What *is* clear is that the
extraordinarily diverse, not to say contradictory, critical
response to *Andorra* suggests that it is not only Max Frisch who
has fallen victim to 'Ratlosigkeit', but some of his critics too.

On the question of *Andorra* representing a model, it was
perhaps expecting a good deal of a Swiss or German audience
not to relate the play exclusively to their own countries. And as
far as Switzerland is concerned, Frisch has never made — in his
Tagebuch 1946-1949 and elsewhere — any secret of the fact that
he finds his fellow countrymen's arrogant conviction, that the
disease of fascism which struck Germany could not infect their
own model democracy, both dangerous and reprehensible. In
Zurich and on other Swiss stages, *Andorra* was thus naturally
assumed to be Switzerland, in the same way that Gottfried
Keller's Seldwyla stood for nineteenth-century Zurich and
Friedrich Dürrenmatt's Güllen (the setting for *Der Besuch der
alten Dame*) was taken as an obvious satire on Swiss society.
Yet, as the reviews of the triple première indicate, the waves of
applause at the final curtain did not suggest a public unmasked
and brought to account for its collective amnesia. Siegfried
Melchinger, for example, wrote in the *Süddeutsche Zeitung* (4
November 1961) of 'den spontanen Applaus der Nicht-
betroffenen' in Zurich and hoped that when the Germans saw
the play they would not find it so easy to contend with. He con-
cluded pointedly: 'Dieser Prozeß spielt in Andorra. Aber
Eichmann war nicht in Andorra' (*55*, p.169). Similarly, in *Die
Welt* (6 November 1961) Friedrich Luft commented wrily:
'Frisch wurde endlos gefeiert. Wird man ihn ebenso verstehen
wie bejubeln?' (*43*, p.43). The history of the play in Switzerland
since the Zurich première provides no encouraging answer; for,
although it rapidly became a prescribed text in schools, *Andorra*
quickly disappeared from the professional stage.

The play's ineffectual strategy in disturbing the Swiss
bourgeois conscience can be discerned to a certain extent by the
interesting preface that Walther Matthias Diggelmann appended
to his controversial novel, *Die Hinterlassenschaft* (1965), which
brought into the open the activities of the Swiss National Front

during the war, and the latent anti-Semitism of the country's
official refugee policy:

> Auch wenn diese Geschichte in der Schweiz spielt, ist sie
> weder als Anklage gegen die Schweizer gedacht noch als
> Exkulpierung jener Deutschen, die sich am Massenmord
> beteiligt haben. Als Schweizer Bürger, der in der Schweiz
> lebt und dieses Land beim Namen nennt, statt eine Parabel
> zu konstruieren, meine ich aber auch, daß die größere
> Schuld die kleinere nicht kleiner mache.

Diggelmann clearly felt that Frisch's parable was weak precisely
because it avoided particularity. His dismissive reference to
Frisch's play, however, ignores the fact that it was *Andorra*
above all which helped to give a whole younger generation of
Swiss writers the confidence to tackle the taboos of post-war
Swiss society, of which development his own novel is the most
conspicuous example.

The reception in Germany of *Andorra* — perhaps not
unexpectedly — was both more thoughtful and more complex.
But the Germans, like the Swiss, tended to ignore the central
point of the play and narrow its focus to their own immediate
past. Writing in *Die Zeit* (26 January 1962), R.W. Leonhardt
summed up the general feeling in uncompromising fashion: 'Das
historische Modell für *Andorra* ist Deutschland.' This view was
taken to its logical conclusion in Peter Palitzsch's Stuttgart production in which he wilfully ignored the author's stage directions
and set the play unequivocally in a small German town and
made his 'Blacks' into an all too readily recognisable reminder
of Germany's fascist past. Under such treatment the parable was
inevitably reduced to the limited dimensions of a *Zeitstück*.

Despite such distortions, however, the initial progress of
Andorra on the West German stage was spectacular. In the
1962/63 season the play received over 900 performances in more
than 70 professional theatres, a record surpassed, interestingly
enough, only by Frisch's compatriot Friedrich Dürrenmatt,
whose *Die Physiker* was played over 1,500 times in the same
period. The contemporary Swiss theatre has never before or

since achieved such a commanding position on the German stage.

Johannes Jacobi, writing in *Die Zeit* (30 March 1962), surveyed the initial response to the play in Munich, Frankfurt, Düsseldorf, Hamburg and Berlin. Whereas in Munich Frisch was greeted by one spectator with the remark: 'Eine typisch eidgenössische Überheblichkeit, so etwas aufzugreifen', the reaction in general 'äußerte sich in Berlin diskreter als in Düsseldorf, wo bei der Premiere einige Leute, als sie gingen, die Türen zuschlugen; anders auch als in Frankfurt am Main, wo nach der Premiere einzelne Buh-Rufe zu hören waren. Aus dem prominenten Berliner Premierenpublikum stahlen sich die Ablehnenden in der Pause hinweg. Die übergroße Mehrheit raffte sich am Ende des Stücks nur zaghaft zum Applaus auf. Man erlebte einen der seltenen Augenblicke, wo Theater mehr als Spiel und 'Kunstgenuß' geworden war. Nach einer Weile der Benommenheit steigerte sich der Beifall dann zum Dank für eine große Leistung'. It was perhaps inevitable that a play ostensibly focussed on anti-Semitism should have been understood in Germany as a drama specifically about their own recent past. In such a situation it was certainly not easy for any critic to utter publicly major doubts either about the moral stance of its author or about the play's aesthetic quality.

No such inhibitions, however, prevented some harsh criticism from Austria. Although *Andorra* there, too, achieved success at the box office, two critics in particular, Hans Weigel and Fritz Torberg, voiced serious reservations. Weigel, indeed, went so far as to declare *Andorra* a dangerous play precisely because it benefitted from the taboo status of its subject. To criticise *Andorra* was to risk being charged as anti-Semitic. But above all he objected to what in his view was an indefensible reduction of the complex problem of fascism to the persecution of the Jews. In the Viennese *Illustrierte Kronen-Zeitung* (31 March 1962) he declared: 'Eine ganze "schwarze" Armee besetzt Andorra, sie marschiert lediglich auf, um den einen "anderen" zu liquidieren, dann zieht sie weiter, und "Wer kein Jud ist, ist frei!" So einfach darf man sich's nicht machen!' (*55*, p.228). The suggestion, he argues, that fascism peacefully disappears after the 'totale Endlösung' is a gross falsification of history. Ironically, Weigel's main objection to the over-simplification of a complex problem could with equal justification be levelled at his own misreading of the play.

A more subtle criticism came from Fritz Torberg who, whilst recognising *Andorra*'s significance, saw the play's central weakness as located in its very flexibility — that quality, of course, which enabled the Swiss and the Germans to see the play as a reflection exclusively of themselves. In his review in *Das Forum* he questioned the legitimacy of using the historical phenomenon of anti-Semitism as a *model* to illustrate the danger of any other kind of prejudice. As a Jew, Torberg could not accept that the tragic fate of Central European Jewry could, even symbolically, be interchangeable with that of other threatened minorities, such as Hans Magnus Enzensberger (paraphrasing Sartre) had suggested in his programme note for the Zurich première ('Kommunist oder Kapitalist oder Gelber, Weißer, Schwarzer, je nachdem'; *25*, pp.274-75). For a Jew confronted with the unimaginable horror of Auschwitz, Torberg's view is readily understandable. However, such criticism unfortunately diverts attention away from what Frisch wrote to what, in the critic's view, he should have written. Nevertheless, Frisch himself certainly anticipated such a reaction, indeed was worried by its possibility, as can be seen in the letter dated 2 March 1962 to Fritz Kortner, the Jewish director of the Schiller Theater production in Berlin:

> *Andorra* ist ja ein Judenstück für die Nichtjuden; während der langen und schwierigen Arbeit hatte ich oft Sorge, nicht daß die Mörder es mir nicht abnehmen, das ist nicht mein Verlangen, aber daß die Juden (die ja von sich aus mehr sind als nur eine Fiktion der Nichtjuden) sich dagegen verwehren. (*MFA*)

Andorra was subsequently performed in Israel to appreciative audiences, and the fact that Frisch was awarded the Jerusalem Prize in 1965 and thus became the first German-speaker to give a speech in Israel in that language since the State's foundation, seems to confirm that Frisch's fears were groundless and Torberg's position an isolated one.

The most curious episode in the early reception of the play, however, had nothing to do with actual performances. In 1963 the Austrian cabarettist Georg Kreisler published a parody of Frisch's play with the title *Sodom und Andorra*. The piece, in fact, has little merit. It turns principally on constant comic reversals of Frisch's scenes, but employs such a heavy-handed wit that the whole concept falls flat.[10] That such a play should be written at all would seem to counter Hans Weigel's concern over the 'danger' of *Andorra* — even though Kreisler had to publish his text in the relatively unknown Estam Verlag in Schaan/Liechtenstein. However, the parody certainly indicates the vigorous impact Frisch's play made in the German-speaking countries, much as Friedrich Nicolai's infamous *Die Freuden des jungen Werthers* once did in relationship to Goethe's masterpiece. In both cases the extravagance of the attack paid its target the highest of all compliments.

In England, Lindsay Anderson's production for the National Theatre in 1964 had no hesitation in underlining the exemplary nature of anti-Semitism as an illustration of the lethal nature of prejudice. The programme, for example, carried photographs of other archetypal outsiders of bourgeois society: Oscar Wilde, the Homosexual; Dylan Thomas, the Alcoholic *Poète Maudit*; Marilyn Monroe, the Universal Sex Object. Anderson wished to stress society's constant need for eccentric individuals onto which it can project its secret fears and shabby rancour. The production achieved a modest *succès d'estime*, the main criticism being focussed on what was seen as the imperfect fusion of Brecht and Ibsen; but like *Biedermann und die Brandstifter* before it, *Andorra* succumbed to the insularity of British taste and vanished from the repertoire almost as soon as it arrived.

At least London did not show the total rejection of New York where the play was a disastrous flop and taken off after only nine performances. The reasons for this failure were complex,

[10] See Curt Riess's dismissive review, 'Antisemitismus als Jux', *Die Zeit*, 25 January 1963.

and certainly not to do entirely with the acknowledged weaknesses of the play itself. Firstly, the play's principal quality, its language, was not accurately reproduced in George Tabori's translation, and secondly, his unhappy adaptation was apparently not helped by the confused direction of Michael Langham. But above all, the play's collapse was due to several extraneous factors. The Biltmore Theatre on Broadway, for example, was hardly the most propitious venue for a play of *Andorra*'s scope, for that institution's insatiable appetite for commercialised entertainment augured ill for any work which tried to raise the profound issues that concerned Frisch. Furthermore, the New York audience appeared incapable of grasping Frisch's characteristic irony which was misinterpreted as cold cynicism. The situation was not helped by the American preference for conventional realism in the theatre: the symbolism and abstractions of Frisch's drama were felt to be 'Teutonic' and unconvincing. More significantly, the relevance to American concerns of a play so rooted in European experience seemed too remote — despite the fact that New York's population has the highest percentage of Jews outside Israel, many of whom had direct experience of Hitler's pogroms. Apparently, the power of the American Dream was still too strong. As one critic put it: 'Das Menetekel, das Frisch in *Andorra* setzt, gilt nichts in einem Lande, in dem das aufgeklärte Bild vom Menschen noch immer allerorten vorherrscht' (*55*, p.247). Yet ironically enough, America stood at that time on the brink of the Vietnam nightmare and in a few months President Kennedy would be dead. It should have proved an excellent sounding-board for the short-sighted arrogance of Frisch's model Andorrans.

The failure of *Andorra* in America, in fact, marked the beginning of an abrupt decline in the play's fortunes also in Europe as far as theatrical productions were concerned. From the mid-1960s the play effectively disappeared from the repertoire as the new trend towards documentary drama began to dominate the German stage. In particular, Rolf Hochhuth's *Der Stellvertreter* (1963) and Peter Weiss's *Die Ermittlung* (1965) appeared to offer an objective dramaturgical method which was more suited than Frisch's sceptical parables to concrete revelations of man's inhumanity to man. Significantly, Frisch himself turned to narrative fiction and other artistic matters. In the purely academic sphere, however, the play — indeed Frisch's theatre as a whole — has never lost its fascination. Monographs, dissertations and scholarly articles continued to be devoted in large numbers to Frisch's work, reaching a peak in the latter half of the 1970s with Suhrkamp's publication of the *Gesammelte Werke in zeitlicher Folge* (1976) which had the effect of conferring an unmistakeable 'classical' status on Frisch's *œuvre*. In the case of *Andorra*, Peter Pütz's stimulating article, 'Max Frischs *Andorra* — ein Modell der Mißverständnisse', published in 1975 in a special number of the periodical *Text + Kritik*, devoted to Max Frisch, marked a turning point in the reception of the play; for Pütz's sensitive analysis rescued the play from fifteen years of misconception. The two *Materialienbände* edited by Wolfgang Frühwald and Walter Schmitz (1977) and by Ernst Wendt and Walter Schmitz (1978) subsequently ensured that *Andorra* could no longer be treated either as an elementary dissection of anti-Semitism or as an out-of-date *Zeitstück*. A work which had languished as a sixth-form set text in most German schools (and not a few English ones!), exhibiting all the features of what Frisch himself once called (in reference to Brecht) 'die durchschlagende Wirkungslosigkeit eines Klassikers' (V, 342), was thoroughly dusted down, its subtleties freshly perceived and its message recognised as possessing a contemporary urgency to match that of the 1960s. Pütz's central point that *Andorra* demonstrates not so much a coming to terms with the past as the recognition that such heart-searching has not yet even begun, has reissued a challenge to theatre directors, critics and audiences alike.

Biographical Sketch

1911	Born 15 May in Zurich. Father: Franz Bruno Frisch (Architect), Mother: Karolina Bettina (née Wildermuth).
1924-30	Realgymnasium, Zurich.
1931	Matriculates at Zurich University to read German.
1932	Father dies. Leaves university to work as freelance journalist.
1933	Travels abroad for first time: Prague, Budapest, Belgrade, Istanbul, Athens, Rome.
1934	*Jürg Reinhart: eine sommerliche Schicksalsfahrt* (novel).
1935	First visit to Germany.
1936-41	Reads architecture at the Eidgenössische Technische Hochschule, Zurich.
1937	*Antwort aus der Stille: eine Erzählung aus den Bergen* (short novel). Decides to give up writing.
1939-45	Several periods of military service (artillery).
1940	*Blätter aus dem Brotsack* (diary).
1941	Qualifies as architect.
1942	Wins competition to construct swimming pool in Zurich (Letzigraben) and opens own architect's office. Marries Constanze von Meyerburg.
1943	*J'adore ce qui me brûle oder Die Schwierigen* (novel).
1944	*Santa Cruz: eine Romanze.*
1945	*Bin oder Die Reise nach Peking* (short story). *Nun singen sie wieder: Versuch eines Requiems.*
1946	*Die Chinesische Mauer: eine Farce.* Travels in Germany, Italy, France.
1947	*Tagebuch mit Marion* (diary). Meets Peter Suhrkamp and Bertolt Brecht.
1948	Visits Prague, Berlin, Warsaw and Breslau (as participant in World Congress of Intellectuals for Peace).

1949	*Als der Krieg zu Ende war: Schauspiel.*
1950	*Tagebuch 1946-1949* (diary).
1951-52	*Graf Öderland: eine Moritat.* First visit to the USA and Mexico.
1953	*Don Juan oder Die Liebe zur Geometrie: Komödie.*
1954	*Stiller* (novel). Separates from wife. Gives up architectural practice.
1955	*achtung: Die Schweiz* (pamphlet).
1956	Travels in USA, Mexico, Cuba.
1957	*Homo Faber* (novel). Travels in the Middle East.
1958	*Biedermann und die Brandstifter: ein Lehrstück ohne Lehre. Die große Wut des Philipp Hotz: ein Schwank.*
1959	Divorces wife.
1960-65	Lives in Rome. Meets Ingeborg Bachmann.
1961	*Andorra.*
1962	Honorary doctorate of Marburg University.
1964	*Mein Name sei Gantenbein* (novel).
1965	Lives in the Ticino (Valle Onsernone), Switzerland. Visits Israel.
1966	*Zürich-Transit: Skizze eines Films.* First visit to the Soviet Union. Visits Poland.
1967	*Öffentlichkeit als Partner* (essays and speeches). *Biografie: ein Spiel.*
1968	Marries Marianne Oellers. Second visit to the Soviet Union. Political activity in Zurich.
1969	*Dramaturgisches: ein Briefwechsel mit Walter Höllerer.* Visits Japan.
1970	Visits USA.
1971	*Wilhelm Tell für die Schule.* Visits USA. Lectures at Columbia University, New York.
1972	*Tagebuch 1966-1971* (diary). Visits USA.
1974	*Dienstbüchlein* (memoir of military service). Elected Honorary Member of American Academy of Arts and Letters and National Institute of Arts and Letters.
1975	*Montauk: eine Erzählung.* Visit to China with West German delegation led by Chancellor Helmut Schmidt.

1976   *Gesammelte Werke in zeitlicher Folge.*
1977   Speech to the SPD Party Conference in Hamburg.
1978   *Triptychon: drei szenische Bilder. Der Traum des Apothekers von Locarno (=stories from the Tagebuch 1966-1971).*
1979   *Der Mensch erscheint im Holozän: eine Erzählung* (short story). Divorces Marianne Oellers. Foundation of the Max Frisch Archive in the Eidgenössische Technische Hochschule, Zurich.
1981   Lives in New York. Proposal for Honorary Doctorate of the Eidgenössische Technische Hochschule blocked.
1982   *Blaubart: eine Erzählung* (short story). Honorary Doctorate of the City University of New York.
1983   Settles in Zurich. *Forderungen des Tages: Porträts, Skizzen, Reden 1943-1982.*
1985   Honorary Doctorate of Letters, University of Birmingham (illness prevents conferment of the degree).
1986   'Am Ende der Aufklärung steht das Goldene Kalb' (='Solothurner Rede').
1989   *Schweiz ohne Armee? Ein Palaver* (stage version, 19-20 October: 'Jonas und sein Veteran', co-produced in the Zurich Schauspielhaus and, in French translation, in the Théâtre de Vidy, Lausanne).
1990   *Schweiz als Heimat? Versuche über 50 Jahre* (contains the 'Solothurner Rede').
1991   4 April: Max Frisch dies in Zurich.

Select Bibliography

A. PRIMARY LITERATURE

Gesammelte Werke in zeitlicher Folge, ed. Hans Mayer and Walter Schmitz (Frankfurt a.m., Suhrkamp, 1976), 6 vols.

Triptychon: drei szenische Bilder (Suhrkamp, 1978, rev. 1980).

Der Mensch erscheint im Holozän: eine Erzählung (Suhrkamp, 1979).

Blaubart: eine Erzählung (Suhrkamp, 1982).

Forderungen des Tages: Porträts, Skizzen, Reden 1943-1982, ed. Walter Schmitz (Suhrkamp, 1983).

Schweiz ohne Armee? Ein Palaver (Suhrkamp, 1989).

Schweiz als Heimat? Versuche über 50 Jahre, ed. Walter Obschlager (Suhrkamp, 1990).

B. SECONDARY LITERATURE

Of the vast amount of critical literature devoted to Frisch's work, a representative selection has been made of those books and articles which relate to Frisch's theatre in general and to *Andorra* in particular, or have been specifically referred to in the text. Comprehensive bibliographies can be found in nos. *4, 7, 10, 27, 31, 40* and *55*.

(i) Interviews

1. Arnold, Heinz Ludwig, 'Gespräch mit Max Frisch', *Gespräche mit Schriftstellern* (Munich, Beck, 1975), pp.9-73.
2. Bienek, Horst, 'Max Frisch', *Werkstattgespräche mit Schriftstellern* [Hanser, 1962] (Munich, DTV, 3rd edition, 1976), pp.21-32.
3. Roth, Gerhard, 'Max Frisch: der Dichter in seiner Klause', *Zeit-Magazin*, no. 21, 15 May 1981.

(ii) On Frisch's theatre generally

4. Arnold, Heinz Ludwig (ed.), 'Max Frisch', *Text + Kritik*, 47/48 (Munich, 3rd, enlarged edition, 1983).
5. Bänziger, Hans, *Frisch und Dürrenmatt* [1960] (Bern, Francke, 6th edition, 1971).
5a. —, *Max Frisch: 'Andorra'. Erläuterungen und Dokumente* (Stuttgart, Reclam, 1985).
6. —, *Zwischen Protest und Traditionsbewußtsein: Arbeiten zum Werk und zur gesellschaftlichen Stellung Max Frischs* (Bern, Francke, 1975).
7. Beckermann, Thomas (ed.), *Über Max Frisch* (Frankfurt a.M., Suhrkamp, 1971).
8. *Begegnung: eine Festschrift für Max Frisch zum siebzigsten Geburtstag* (Frankfurt a.M., Suhrkamp, 1981).

9. Biedermann, Marianne, *Das politische Theater von Max Frisch* (Lampertheim, Schäuble, 1974).

10. Butler, Michael, *The Plays of Max Frisch* (London, Macmillan, 1985).

11. Durzak, Manfred, *Dürrenmatt, Frisch, Weiss: deutsches Drama der Gegenwart zwischen Kritik und Utopie* (Stuttgart, Reclam, 1972).

12. Frisch, Max, *Dramaturgisches: ein Briefwechsel mit Walter Höllerer* (Berlin, Colloquium, 1969).

13. Gontrum, Peter, 'Max Frisch and the Theatre of Bertolt Brecht', *German Life & Letters*, 33, 2 (1980), 163-71.

14. Hage, Volker, *Max Frisch* (Reinbek bei Hamburg, Rowohlt, 1983).

15. Jurgensen, Manfred, *Max Frisch, die Dramen* [1968] (Bern, Francke, 2nd edition, 1976).

16. —— (ed.), *Frisch: Kritik — Thesen — Analysen* (Bern, Francke, 1977).

17. Karasek, Hellmuth, *Max Frisch* [Velber bei Hannover, Friedrich, 1966] (Munich, DTV, 5th edition, 1974).

18. Knapp, Gerhard P. (ed.), *Max Frisch: Aspekte des Bühnenwerks* (Bern, Lang, 1979).

19. Matthias, Klaus, 'Die Dramen von Max Frisch: Strukturen und Aussagen', *Literatur in Wissenschaft und Unterricht*, 3 (1970), 129-50 and 236-52. Reprinted in 27, pp.75-124.

20. Mennemeier, Franz Norbert, 'Liberaler Nachkriegshumanismus (Max Frisch)', *Modernes deutsches Drama: Kritiken und Charakteristiken*, Vol. 2 (Munich, Fink, 1975), pp.160-79.

21. Pender, Malcolm, *Max Frisch: his Work and its Swiss Background* (Stuttgart, Heinz, 1979).

22. Petersen, Carol, *Max Frisch* (New York, Ungar, 1972).

23. Petersen, Jürgen H., *Max Frisch* (Stuttgart, Metzler, 1978).

24. Pickar, Gertrud B., *The Dramatic Works of Max Frisch* (Bern, Lang, 1977).

25. Schau, Albrecht (ed.), *Max Frisch: Beiträge zu einer Wirkungsgeschichte* (Freiburg im Breisgau, Becksmann, 1971).

26. Schenker, Walter, *Die Sprache Max Frischs in der Spannung zwischen Mundart und Schriftsprache* (Berlin, de Gruyter, 1969).

27. Schmitz, Walter (ed.), *Über Max Frisch II* (Frankfurt a.M., Suhrkamp, 1976).

28. ——, *Max Frisch: das Werk (1931-1961)*, (Bern, Lang, 1985).

29. Schnetzler-Suter, Annemarie, *Max Frisch: dramaturgische Fragen* (Bern, Lang, 1974).

30. Stephan, Alexander, *Max Frisch* (Munich, Beck, 1983).

31. ——, 'Max Frisch' in Heinz Ludwig Arnold (ed.), *Kritisches Lexikon zur deutschsprachigen Gegenwartsliteratur* (Munich, Edition Text + Kritik, 1982).

32. Weise, Adelheid, *Untersuchungen zur Thematik und Struktur der Dramen von Max Frisch* (Göppingen, Kümmerle, 1975).

33. Weisstein, Ulrich, *Max Frisch* (New York, Twayne, 1967).

34. Wintsch-Spiess, Monika, *Zum Problem der Identität im Werk Max Frischs* (Zurich, Juris, 1965).

(iii) *On* Andorra

35. Arnold, Armin, 'Woyzeck in Andorra: Max Frisch und Georg Büchner', in *18*, pp.297-311.
36. Eckart, Rolf, *Max Frisch: 'Andorra'. Interpretation* (Munich, Oldenbourg, 1965).
37. Enzensberger, Hans Magnus, 'Über *Andorra*', *Programmheft des Schauspielhauses Zürich* (1961-62), 4-7. Reprinted in *25*, pp.274-75.
38. Feinberg, A., '*Andorra* — Twenty Years On', *New German Studies*, 10, 3 (1982), 175-90.
39. Frühwald, Wolfgang, 'Wo ist Andorra? Zu einem poetischen Modell Max Frischs' in *27*, pp.305-13.
40. Frühwald, Wolfgang, and Walter Schmitz (eds), '*Andorra*'/'*Wilhelm Tell*': *Materialien, Kommentare* (Munich, Hanser, 1977).
41. Hegele, Wolfgang, 'Max Frisch: *Andorra*', *Der Deutschunterricht*, 20, 3 (1968), 35-50. Reprinted in *7*, pp.172-91.
42. Hilty, Hans Rudolf, 'Tabu *Andorra*', *DU*, 22, 5 (1962), 52-54. Reprinted in *55*, pp.113-21.
43. Knapp, Gerhard P. and Mona, *Max Frisch: Andorra* (Frankfurt a.M., Diesterweg, 1980).
44. Leo (R.W. Leonhardt), 'Wo liegt Andorra?', *Die Zeit*, 26 January 1962.
45. Michaelis, Rolf, 'Andorra bei uns', *Stuttgarter Zeitung*, 8 May 1962. Reprinted in *55*, pp.209-13.
46. Petermann, Gerd Alfred, 'Max und die Psychologie. Kritische Anmerkungen zu Interpretationen von *Andorra*', in *18*, pp.313-19.
47. Plett, Peter C., *Dokumente zu Max Frischs 'Andorra'* (Stuttgart, Klett, 1972).
48. Pütz, Peter, 'Max Frischs *Andorra* — ein Modell der Mißverständnisse', *Text + Kritik*, 47/48 (1975), 37-43. Reprinted in *55*, pp.122-32.
49. Riess, Curt, 'Mitschuldige sind überall. Eine Unterhaltung mit Max Frisch über sein neues Stück', *Die Zeit*, 3 November 1961.
50. Schmid, Karl, 'Max Frisch: Andorra und die Entscheidung', *Unbehagen im Kleinstaat* [1963] (Zurich, Artemis, 3rd edition, 1977), pp.169-200. Reprinted in *7*, pp.147-71.
51. Schmitz, Walter, 'Max Frischs *Andorra* — als Wirklichkeits- und als Erkenntnismodell', in H. Müller-Michaels (ed.), *Deutsche Dramen: Interpretationen zu Werken von der Aufklärung bis zur Gegenwart*, Vol. 2 (Königstein/Ts., Athenäum, 1981), pp.112-36.
52. Thieberger, Richard, '*Andorra* — nur ein Modell?', in *18*, pp.341-55.
53. Torberg, Friedrich, 'Ein fruchtbares Mißverständnis. Notizen zur Zürcher Uraufführung des Schauspiels *Andorra* von Max Frisch', *Das Forum*, 8 (Vienna, 1961), 455-56. Reprinted in *25*, pp.296-99.
54. Weigel, Hans, 'Warnung vor *Andorra*', *Illustrierte Kronen-Zeitung*, 31 March 1962. Reprinted in *55*, pp.225-29.

55. Wendt, Ernst, and Walter Schmitz (eds), *Materialien zu Max Frischs 'Andorra'* (Frankfurt a.M., Suhrkamp, 1978).
56. Wysling, Hans, 'Dramaturgische Probleme in Frischs *Andorra* und Dürrenmatts *Der Besuch der alten Dame*', in *Akten des V.Internationalen Germanisten-Kongresses* (Cambridge, 1975), pp.425-31. Reprinted in *55*, pp.133-42.